DEVELOPING READING SKILLS: BEGINNING

SECOND EDITION

Linda Markstein

Borough of Manhattan Community College
The City University of New York
New York, New York

HEINLE & HEINLE PUBLISHERS
A Division of Wadsworth, Inc.
Boston, Massachusetts 02116

The publication of *Developing Reading Skills; Beginning, second edition* was directed by the members of the Newbury House Publishing Team at Heinle & Heinle:

Erik Gundersen, Editorial Director
John McHugh, Market Development Director
Gabrielle B. McDonald, Production Editor

Also participating in the publication of this program were:

Publisher: Stanley J. Galek
Editorial Production Manager: Elizabeth Holthaus
Project Manager: Carole Rollins
Assistant Editor: Karen P. Hazar
Associate Marketing Manager: Donna Hamilton
Production Assistant: Maryellen Eschmann
Manufacturing Coordinator: Mary Beth Lynch
Photo Coordinator: Martha Leibs-Heckly
Cover Designer: Kimberly Wedlake

Heinle & Heinle Publishers is a division of Wadsworth, Inc.

Manufactured in the United States of America

For permission to use copyrighted text, photos, and illustrations, grateful acknowledgment to the copyright holders is given on pages 192 and 193, which are hereby made part of the copyright page.

Library of Congress Cataloging in Publication Data

Markstein, Linda.
   Developing reading skills. Beginning / Linda Markstein.—2nd ed.
   p.   cm.
   ISBN 0-8384-4987-5
   1. English language—Textbooks for foreign speakers.   2. Readers.
I. Title.
PE1128.M3445   1994   93-45815
428.6′4—dc20   CIP

ISBN: 0-8384-4987-5

10 9 8 7 6 5

CONTENTS

INTRODUCTION

Developing Reading Skills: Beginning, Second Edition, is part of a reading skills development series specially designed for adults and secondary students who are learning English as a second or foreign language. This book is the first level of a developmental reading series that includes:

- ◆ *Developing Reading Skills: Intermediate 1*
- ◆ *Expanding Reading Skills: Intermediate 2*
- ◆ *Developing Reading Skills: Advanced 1*
- ◆ *Expanding Reading Skills: Advanced 2*

Developing Reading Skills: Beginning, Second Edition contains new and updated content since the first edition and additional emphasis on speaking as well as reading and writing skills. A comprehensive Answer Key is available.

General Description

Developing Reading Skills: Beginning, Second Edition contains five units, and each unit has four reading passages that are integrated by a common theme. The themes are cross-cultural in content, and they include:

- ◆ **Names and Naming Customs**
- ◆ **Cities (New York, Beijing, Mexico City)**
- ◆ **Education and Educational Systems (the United States, Saudi Arabia, South Korea)**
- ◆ **Sports**
- ◆ **Superstitions**

Exercises following the passages develop and extend comprehension through a variety of reading, writing, speaking, and listening activities.

Rationale for Materials Design

The materials design for *Developing Reading Skills: Beginning,* Second Edition has been heavily inspired by Jerome Bruner's spiral curriculum model. For the last 40 years, Bruner has repeatedly emphasized two important pedagogical points:

1. Any subject that is worth knowing about can, at some meaningful level, be made accessible to students at any age, or skill level;
2. A topic that is given time and place in the curriculum must be a topic that can be expanded and elaborated so as to be worthy of the serious attention of a thoughtful adult.

These two points have strong implications for ESL/EFL materials design, and they have guided the basic design of these materials.

Bruner's thematic spiral design makes it possible to create ESL/EFL materials worthy of the serious attention of a thoughtful adult. Each unit introduces a theme on a very simple level that is accessible to the beginning-level reader. The exercises following the passage help the reader consolidate and develop meaning. Then, gradually and systematically, the theme is expanded and elaborated in subsequent readings. After each reading, exercises help integrate the latest reading into the reader's prior knowledge base. Finally, the fourth reading is a literary excerpt related to the unit theme from works that include *The House on Mango Street* (Sandra Cisneros), *The Joy Luck Club* (Amy Tan), and *Iron & Silk* (Mark Salzman).

The thematic spiral is a very efficient and effective design for ESL/EFL students because it is constantly recycling and building upon concepts, vocabulary, and structures that have previously been introduced. The end result is that in a relatively short amount of time, beginning students of English are able to read mainstream, unsimplified passages from literature related to the unit theme, and this accomplishment provides them not only with pride but with a powerful incentive to continue their language learning efforts.

Description of Activities

Developing Reading Skills: Beginning, Second Edition, can be flexibly adapted to various instructional modes: individual, pair, small group, and large group depending upon the class instructional objectives. However, whenever possible, it is recommended that pair and small group instruction be used to maximize communication opportunities for each student in the classroom.

Each unit has five major parts and one short wrap-up:

1. Pre-reading discussion questions, first reading passage, and exercises;

2   Second reading passage and exercises;

3. Third reading passage and exercises;

4. Expansion activities: Interview and small group interaction; reporting;

5. Special reading (essay or excerpt from literature) and freewriting;

6. Wrap-up: Analysis of quotations on the theme of the unit.

Approximately ten hours are needed to cover each of the units although there is considerable variation from student to student. Some parts can be assigned as homework.

1. *Pre-reading discussion questions:* These questions are designed to introduce the unit theme to the readers and to help them relate their prior knowledge and experience to the theme. Teachers can ask the questions, or students can ask each other these questions in pairs or small groups.

2. *Reading passages #1, #2, and #3*: It is recommended that each passage be read three times:

First Reading: Getting the Main Idea

Students should be encouraged to read through the entire passage without stopping to look up unfamiliar words in the glossary or in a dictionary. They should be allowed to do the first reading at their own speed, no matter how slow that speed may be. (*Note:* As students progress through the book and increase their knowledge of English vocabulary and structure, their reading speed will naturally increase. The most important point in the first reading is to keep the anxiety level as low as possible.)

Second Reading: Filling in the Gaps

After the students have read through the passage once for the main ideas, they should go back and read the passage a second time. Then, they can work with a partner to look up words in the glossary at the end of the book or in a dictionary. Students should be allowed to use bilingual dictionaries if they wish.

Third Reading: Consolidating Conceptual and Linguistic Information

Finally, the students should read over the passage a third time to consolidate the conceptual and linguistic information from the first two readings and to integrate new words into their contexts. This third reading can gradually be developed into a skimming activity, but we caution teachers not to emphasize speed until the students are ready for this challenge. (*Note:* Some students will be ready sooner than others. If it is possible, these individual differences should be noted and accommodated.)

3. *Understanding Ideas and Vocabulary, Let's Talk!* (a discussion exercise), *Cloze, and Vocabulary and Structure Practice:* Students working together in pairs or small groups derive maximum benefit from these communication activities. *Understanding Ideas and Vocabulary* focuses on identification of main ideas and important details as well as building semantic clusters. General class discussion of answers is recommended. *Let's Talk!*, a guided discussion activity, helps students relate the unit themes and reading selections to their own experience as they did with the pre-reading questions. At this point, however, they can give more expansive answers. The cloze exercise is designed to help students become aware of the semantic and syntactic signals and ties of written discourse. Students can heighten their own linguistic awareness by working in pairs, explaining why certain options work in particular frames and others do not. *Vocabulary and Structure Practice* is a word form exercise that systematically builds vocabulary through developing awareness of common word forms (e.g. common adjective endings such as *-ful* and *-able*).

4. *Interviewing and reporting:* After students have completed the first three readings and follow-up exercises, they interview a classmate or someone outside the class. In the early units, interview questions are suggested although students are always encouraged to adapt or change the questions as they wish. In later units, they are gradually given less direct guidance so they can learn how to develop their own interview formats. They learn how to elicit information through asking questions, one of the most important strategies for any language user. After conducting the interview, students give an oral report about the interview to their own group-mates. This sequence of activities opens up new opportunities for students to practice English in meaningful communication settings. The emphasis at this stage should be upon developing fluency and confidence in speaking rather than on strict accuracy.

5. *Special reading and freewriting:* Students get an end-of-unit bonus of a special reading selection connected to the unit theme. The readings are unadapted excerpts from such works as *The House on Mango Street, The Joy Luck Club,* and *Iron & Silk,*. These readings

have great psychological importance because they dramatically demonstrate the student's new reading power in English, and they complete the materials spiral initiated in the first reading of the unit. The following freewriting allows and encourages the student to draw connections between the reading and their own experience. By this point in the unit, students have much more English at their command to use in their freewritings.

6. *Final quotations:* Each unit ends with famous quotations related to the theme for the students to analyze and discuss. For example, the first unit on names and naming customs ends with the following quotation:

"What's in a name? That which we call a rose
By any other name would smell as sweet."

WILLIAM SHAKESPEARE,
Romeo and Juliet, Act II, scene ii

Glossary: A glossary is included at the end of the book to help students understand and learn new words. In addition, they should be encouraged to use a dictionary as well.

Finally as students work their way through each unit, they are able to feel the joy and power that come from learning a new language and making it their own. Through the spiral, they are able to move beyond the agonizing early language learning stage quickly, and their rapid progress motivates them to continue their language learning efforts on their own.

LINDA MARKSTEIN

Borough of Manhattan Community College
The City University of New York
January, 1994

Names and Naming Customs

Before You Begin

DISCUSS THESE QUESTIONS WITH YOUR CLASSMATES:

1. What is your name?
2. What is your family name? Is it a common name in your country?
3. What is your given name? Does it mean something? If so, what does it mean?
4. Do you like your name? Why or why not?

What's Your Name?

Joanna Medina is in a passport office. She wants to get a new
passport, and she is talking to a passport clerk who is working in the
office. **Read this dialogue with a partner. One of you should read
the lines for the passport clerk, and the other should read the lines
for Joanna.**

Clerk: Good morning. May I help you?

Joanna: Yes, please. I would like to get a passport.

Clerk: Yes. Do you already have a passport? Do you want **to renew**
            your old passport or to get a new one?

Joanna: To get a new one. I've never had one before.

Clerk: All right. Just fill out these papers, please. Start off with your
            name: last name, first name, and your middle name or
            initial. Be sure to print clearly.

Joanna: Okay. Last name first?

Clerk: Yes, write your family name first and then your given name
            or names. You can go over to that desk **to fill out** these
            papers. If you need any help, please come back.

Joanna: Thank you. [She goes over to a desk across the room and
            begins filling out the **application**.]

First Reading: Getting the Main Idea

Read through the following passage. Try to understand the meaning,
and don't stop to look up new words. Take as much time as you need
to complete your first reading.

UNITED STATES DEPARTMENT OF STATE
APPLICATION FOR PASSPORT BY MAIL

TYPE OR PRINT IN INK IN WHITE AREAS ONLY   USE BLOCK LETTERS/NUMBERS

NAME	FIRST		MIDDLE
LAST			

MAIL PASSPORT TO

STREET / RFD # OR P.O. BOX		APT. #
CITY	STATE	ZIP CODE

IN CARE OF (IF APPLICABLE)

R   D   O   DP   Issue Date _____

End.# _____   Exp. _____

SEX	PLACE OF BIRTH		DATE OF BIRTH	SOCIAL SECURITY NUMBER (SEE FEDERAL TAX LAW NOTICE ON REVERSE SIDE)
☐ Male ☐ Female	City & State or City & Country		Month Day Year	

FOLD

HEIGHT Feet Inches	HAIR COLOR	EYE COLOR	HOME TELEPHONE ( )	BUSINESS TELEPHONE ( )

NOTE: Most recent passport MUST be enclosed!

PASSPORT NUMBER	ISSUE DATE Month Day Year	PLACE OF ISSUANCE	OCCUPATION (Not Mandatory)

DEPARTURE DATE	COUNTRIES TO BE VISITED	TRAVEL PLANS (Not Mandatory)	LENGTH OF STAY (Not Mandatory)

PERMANENT ADDRESS (Do not list P.O.Box)

STREET / R.F.D. #	CITY	STATE	ZIP CODE

NOT MANDATORY

IN CASE OF EMERGENCY WHEN TRAVELING ABROAD, NOTIFY (Person in U.S. Not Traveling With You)

NAME
STREET

CITY	STATE	ZIP CODE

TELEPHONE ( )	RELATIONSHIP

2" X 2"   FROM 1" TO 1-3/8"

SUBMIT TWO RECENT IDENTICAL PHOTOS WITH LIGHT, PLAIN BACKGROUND

OATH AND SIGNATURE (If any of the below-mentioned acts or conditions have been performed by or apply to the applicant the portion which applies should be lined out, and a supplementary explanatory statement should be attached, signed, and made a part of this application.)

I have not, since acquiring United States citizenship, been naturalized as a citizen of a foreign state; taken an oath, or made an affirmation or other formal declaration of allegiance to a foreign state; entered or served in the armed forces of a foreign state; accepted or performed the duties of any office, post, or employment under the Government of a foreign state or political subdivision thereof; made a formal renunciation of nationality either in the United States or before a diplomatic or consular officer of the United States in a foreign state; or been convicted by a court or court martial of competent jurisdiction of committing any act of treason against, or attempting by force to overthrow, or bearing arms against the United States, or conspiring to overthrow, put down or destroy by force the Government of the United States.

WARNING: False statements made knowingly and willfully in passport applications or affidavits or other supporting documents are punishable by fine and/or imprisonment under the provisions of 18 USC 1001 and/or 18 USC 1542. The alteration or mutilation of a passport issued pursuant to this application is punishable by fine and/or imprisonment under 18 USC 1543. The use of a passport in violation of the restrictions therein is punishable by fine and/or imprisonment under 18 USC 1544.

DECLARATION: I declare that the statements made in this application are true and complete to the best of my knowledge and belief, that the attached photographs are a true likeness of me, and that I have not been issued or included in a passport issued subsequent to the one submitted herein.

FOLD

➤ **NOTE: APPLICANT MUST SIGN & DATE**

SIGNATURE	DATE

DO NOT WRITE BELOW THIS SPACE – FOR PASSPORT SERVICES USE ONLY – DO NOT WRITE BELOW THIS SPACE

Application Approval	Evidence of Name Change ☐ Marriage Cert. ☐ Court Order	Fees
	Date _____ Place _____ From _____ To _____	

FORM DSP-82 (2-93)

OMB No. 1405-0020 (Exp. 7/31/93) Estimated Burden – 5 Minutes*

Names Are Important

Names are important. The first thing you want to know about people is their name. When you go to school, to apply for a job, or to get a passport as Joanna did, usually the first question is "What's your name?"

Everyone in the world has a name, and most people have two or more names. For example, they have a family name, and they also have one or more given names. Gonzales, Jones, and Chang are examples of family names. Reynaldo, Anne, and Mei are examples of given names.

Every society has its own **customs** about names and how they are used. These customs are not the same in all societies. In many countries, people write or say their family name first and then their given names. For example,

Shin Po Kwun

The family name here is "Shin," and the given names are "Po Kwun." This is a Chinese name, and the custom in China is to write or say the family name first and then the given names after. This is also the custom in Japan, Korea, Vietnam, and in many other countries around the world.

In English-speaking countries such as England, Canada, and the United States, people usually say their given name (or names) first and then their family name. For example,

Michael Jordan
Hillary Clinton

"Michael" and "Hillary" are given names, and "Jordan" and "Clinton" are family names. However, when people have to fill out forms (applications, for example), they are sometimes asked to write their family name first and then their given names, just as Joanna did when she filled out her passport application.

Family Names

In most countries, the family name is the father's family name. For example, if the father's family name is Odabashian, then the family name is also Odabashian. If the father's family name is Han, then the family name is Han.

In some countries, the mother's family name is also part of the child's family name. This is true in Spain and other Spanish-speaking countries. Look at the picture above. This little boy's name is José. His father's name is Fernández, and his mother's family name is Clemente. Therefore, José's family name is Fernández Clemente and his full name is José Fernández Clemente.

Look at this list of the most **common** names in the United States in 1770, more than 200 years ago:

1. Smith
2. Jones

3. Brown
4. Williams
5. Allen

Now look at this list of the most common family names in the United States today:

1. Smith
2. Johnson
3. Williams
4. Brown
5. Jones

As you can see, most of the popular family names from 1770 are still popular in the United States today, more than 200 years later.

The most common family names of Hispanic-Americans[1] (people who came to America from a Spanish-speaking country) in the United States are these:

1.	Rodríguez	6.	Hernández
2.	González	7.	Pérez
3.	García	8.	Sánchez
4.	López	9.	Torres
5.	Rivera	10.	Ortiz

What is the most common family name in the world? The answer is Chang. Chang is a Chinese name, and it means "always" or "all the time." In Korea, the most common family name is Kim, which means "gold." Other common Korean names are Rhee, Ahn, and Park. In Vietnam, the most common family name is Tran. Other common Vietnamese family names are Nguyen, Thieu, and Van.

In English-speaking cultures, people often say *last name* instead of *family name* because *last name* and *family name* mean the same thing in these cultures. *Surname* also means last or family name.

(609 words)

---

[1] **Hispanic-Americans** are also called "Latinos".

Second Reading: Filling in the Gaps

Read the passage a second time to help you understand it better. After you finish the second reading, work with another student in your class and try to guess the meanings of new words. You and your partner should try to decide what the words mean by looking at the context (other words and sentences around the new word). After you have tried to guess the meanings of the new words, look them up in the glossary of this book, or look them up in a dictionary.

Third Reading: Putting the Information Together

Read the passage a third time as quickly as you can. Try to understand the meaning of the new words in their context as you read. Reading the passage a third time will help you understand the ideas and learn new vocabulary at the same time.

1. Understanding Ideas and Vocabulary

Draw a circle around the letter of the **best** answer. Talk about your answers with your classmates.

1. "The most common name in the world is Chang." This means

   a. many people in the world have this name.
   b. a few people in the world have this name.
   c. many people like this name.

2. What does the name Kim mean?

   a. Korean
   b. Gold
   c. Always

3. What language does a Hispanic-American speak besides English?

   a. English
   b. Spanish
   c. Arabic

4. In English-speaking countries, how do people usually say their names?

   a. Family name and then given names: *Jones Jennifer Sue*

    b.   Given names and then family name: *Jennifer Sue Jones*

    c.   With both the mother's and the father's family names: *Jennifer Jones Smith*

5.   In English-speaking countries, people often say *last name* when they mean

    a.   the given name.

    b.   the first name.

    c.   the family name.

2. Let's Talk!

These questions ask you about family names in your culture. Talk about your answers with two or three of your classmates. After you finish talking, write your answers on the blank lines.

1.   What is your family name? _____

2.   What is your given name? _____

    Do you have more than one given name? If so, what are your

    other given names? _____

3.   In your country, do people usually write their given name or their

    family name first? _____

4.   Write your full name here, and then tell the other students in your group your given name and your family name.

    _____

5.   What are five of the most common family names in your country?

    _____

    _____

    _____

    _____

3. Vocabulary and Structure Practice

Choose the correct word and write it on the line. Talk about your answers with your group.

Names and naming customs are very interesting. Every

society _____ (1) has its own *customs* _____ (2) for
person—society—city   *customs—reasons—times*

giving people names. These customs are not the _____ (3)
                                        different—same—best

in all _____ (4). For example, in some
      countries—cities—ways

_____ (5), people write their given name first. Then
countries—cities—ways

they write their _____ (6) name last. In other
                given—first—family

_____ (7), people write their family name first, and
words—cities—countries

after their family name, they write their _____ (8)
                                          family—given—father's

name. In Spanish-speaking countries, people write both their

father's family name and their mother's _____ (9)
                                        given—family—father's

name. The most _____ (10) family name in
               common—important—unusual

the world is Chang.

A christening ceremony in West Virginia

Given Names

R ebecca Chow meets an old classmate from school at a park. They haven't seen each other for five years, and the classmate now has a baby boy. **Read this dialogue with a partner. One of you should read the lines for Rebecca and the other should read the lines for Sarah.**

Rebecca: Sarah! What a **surprise**! I haven't seen you in at least five or six years!

Sarah: Rebecca! Rebecca Chow! You look just the same as you did in high school. You haven't changed!

Rebecca: Oh, oh. Is that good or bad? (laughing)

Sarah: Good! You look great, as a matter of fact.

Rebecca: So do you. And the baby! This can't be your baby!

Sarah: Oh, yes, it can!

Rebecca: I can't believe it! You have a baby?

Sarah: Yeah, I got married a couple of years ago. Remember Sam Martin, the guy I used to like in high school? We didn't **date** then, but later on we got together...and, well, here we are, married and with a new baby!

Rebecca: I can't believe it! I really can't! You, married with a baby! And what an **adorable** baby! Is it a boy or a girl? I'm sorry, but I can't tell at this age.

Sarah: It's a boy. Sammy. Well, his real name is Samuel David Martin. He's **named** after his father, Sam, and my father, David.

Rebecca: Samuel David Martin. That's a big name for such a little person!

Sarah: Yeah! So we call him Sammy. That **fits** him a little better for now.

First Reading: Getting the Main Idea

Read through the following passage. Try to understand the meaning, and don't stop to look up new words. Take as much time as you need to complete your first reading.

Namesakes

Sarah said that her baby is named after his father and his grandfather: Samuel (father's name) David (grandfather's name). People sometimes give a baby the name (or names) of someone who is important to them in some way, and we say then that the baby is named after that person. If you were named after someone, you are that person's **namesake**. Samuel David is the namesake of both his father and his grandfather, for example. It is a great **honor** to have someone named after you because it means that the parents love and **respect** you very much, and they want their child to be like you.

Sometimes people name their children after famous people. In the 1980s, many parents named their daughters Diana, after Diana, the princess of Wales in Great Britain. In the 1960s and 1970s, many little boys around the world were named Elvis, after Elvis Presley, the famous rock and roll singer.

Who Names the Baby?

Naming customs are not the same in all societies. In some societies, for example, the parents (father and the mother) name the baby together. In other societies, someone else names the baby—the grandparents or the godmother and godfather (special friends or family members chosen by the parents). In Greece, the godmother or godfather names the baby, and the parents do not even know the baby's name until it is announced at a religious **ceremony** at the church!

In some societies, children have two given names. All of the girls or boys in a family may have the same first name and a different second name. For example, all of the girls may have the name Marie as the first given name with a different second given name: Marie-Rose, Marie-Jeanne, Marie-Christine. All the boys may have the same first name Jean with different second names: Jean-Paul, Jean Christophe, Jean-Pierre.

Religious Names

In some cultures, people have a religious name. Roman Catholics and Greek Orthodox cultures use the names of saints for their children: Teresa (St. Teresa), Anthony (St. Anthony), Nikos (St. Nicholas). Jews often choose names from the Bible, such as Adam, Rebecca, David. Muslims choose names from the **Koran** such as Mohammed and Ali.

The Meanings of Given Names

In some cultures, people give children names with special meanings to bring the children good luck and fortune. For example, a Chinese family might name a baby Po Lok. Po means "good," and Lok means "happiness" or "joy." We can guess that the family hopes that names with such **positive** meanings will bring the child **good luck** in life.

Restrictions on Given Names

In some countries, a child must have a **traditional** name from that culture. For example, in France and Belgium, parents have to choose a common name from the past. Once a couple (a man and a woman) in France wanted to name their daughter Daisy, but they could not because Daisy is not a traditional French name.

In other countries, however, you can give your child any name you choose. There are no **restrictions** on names at all. In the United States, for example, parents are free to name their child any name, and they can even make up a new name if they want. We can see in birth records some interesting and amusing examples of this freedom in choosing names. In the state of Pennsylvania, the birth records show that one child was named Pepsi and another was named Coke. In Mississippi, a baby girl was named Glory Halleluiah. In another state, a couple had five sons before, at last, they had a daughter. What did they name her? Atlasta—meaning "at last a girl" or "at last we have a girl!"
(670 words)

Second Reading: Filling in the Gaps

Read the passage a second time to help you understand it better. After you finish the second reading, work with another student in your class and try to guess the meanings of new words.

Third Reading: Putting the Information Together

Read the passage a third time as quickly as you can. Try to understand the meaning of the new words in their context as you read. Reading the passage a third time will help you understand the ideas and learn new vocabulary at the same time.

1. Understanding Ideas and Vocabulary

Draw a circle around the letter of the best answer. Talk about your answers with your classmates.

1. In some cultures, people try to choose names with positive meanings for their children because

    a. they are required by law to do this.
    b. they hope these names will bring their children good luck and fortune.
    c. all of the names in the culture have positive meanings, so they have no other choice.

2. Mohammed is a (an) _____ name in Muslim culture.

    a. unusual
    b. common
    c. new

3. Godparents are especially important in Greek society because

    a. they have the responsibility of naming the child.
    b. they usually have an important position and a lot of money.
    c. they have a special relationship with the parents.

4. Match these words. Draw a line from the words on the left to the words on the right that mean almost the same thing.

    1. uncle   a. boys
    2. daughters   b. mother's or father's brother
    3. aunt   c. mother's or father's sister
    4. sons   d. mother and father
    5. parents   e. girls

5. Some of these statements are true, and some of them are not true. Read each statement carefully, and then write **true** or **false** in each blank.

  _____ a. People in the United States are required to give their children traditional names.

  _____ b. If you have a namesake, you have someone named after you.

  _____ c. Godparents are always related to one of the parents.

  _____ d. Naming customs are the same in all societies.

  _____ e. Parents in France often create new names for their children.

2. Let's Talk!

These questions ask you about naming customs in your culture. Talk about your answers with two or three of your classmates. After you finish talking, write your answers on the blank lines.

1. Who usually names children in your culture?

  _____

2. Who named you? _____

3. Does your name have a special meaning? If so, what does it

  mean? _____

  _____

4. Are there any special or unusual customs for naming children in your culture? If so, what are these customs?

  _____

  _____

  _____

  _____

5. What are some of the most common given names in your culture?

For girls: _____ , _____ , _____

For boys: _____ , _____ , _____

Are these religious names, or do they have any special meaning? If so, please explain.

6. Do you have children? If so, how did you choose their names?

_____

_____

_____

3. Vocabulary and Structure Practice

Choose the correct word and write it on the line. Talk about your answers with your group.

Sometimes the parents or the grandparents _____ (1)
like—name—feed

the child. Sometimes, however, the _____ (2)
parents—godparents—grandparents

name the child. Chinese people try to _____ (3) the name
choose—write—say

of a child carefully. The name can have a special meaning, and

they choose a name that is _____ (4). Religious
positive—negative—funny

parents give the child a name from the Koran or the

_____ (5). Roman Catholics name their
telephone book—Bible—friend

children after _____ (6). Sometimes a child is given
movie stars—singers—saints

the name of a special person the child's parents love and respect

very much. This child is the _____ (7) of this
child—namesake—daughter

special person. It is an _____ (8) to have a name-
honor—privilege—mistake
sake. It means the parents love and respect you. In some cultures,

parents have to give children _____ (9) names.
popular—beautiful—traditional
In other cultures, parents are _____ (10) to name their
religious—sad—free
children whatever they want. They can even make up a new name!

Top: Stevie Wonder; bottom left: David Bowie; bottom right: Marilyn Monroe.

Changing Names

This conversation takes place at a student party in Los Angeles between two university students, Joseph Lee and Anne Haddad. **Read this dialogue with a partner. One of you should read the lines for Joseph, and the other should read the lines for Anne.**

Joseph: Hi, weren't we in a class together last summer at UCLA? A **chemistry** class, I think?

Anne: Oh, yeah. It was at 8 in the morning or some terrible hour like that. I'm sorry. I don't remember your name, but I recognized you when I came in.

Joseph: Yeah, I recognized you too. I'm Joseph Lee.

Anne: I'm Anne, Anne Haddad. Nice to see you again.

Joseph: Anne? That's funny. I thought your name was Hanna or Hanan, or something like that.

Anne: That's right. My real name is Hanna, but I changed it. I go by Anne now. It's easier. No one could ever remember my name before. Of course, my family still calls me Hanna.

Joseph: That's interesting. I've been thinking about changing my name too. I think Joseph is too serious for me. It doesn't fit me.

Anne: What about Joe? You could call yourself Joe.

Joseph: No, there are too many Joes in the world. I was thinking about Jay or maybe José. What do you think about José? José Lee.

Anne: José? That's a great idea, especially since you're not Latino![2] That would really be different.

---

[2] **Latino** is a person originally from a Latin American country; Hispanic-American.

Joseph: Yeah, if I were Latino, José would be too common[3]. But, tell me, how many Korean-American guys do you know named José?

Anne: I think you'll be the first.

Joseph: Good! I want to be different. That's my goal.

First Reading: Getting the Main Idea

Read through the following passage. Try to understand the meaning, and don't stop to look up new words. Take as much time as you need to complete your first reading.

Why Do People Change Their Names?

The conversation between Anne and Joseph brings up an interesting question. Why do some people change their names? There can be many reasons. Hanna changed her name to Anne because she thought it would be easier for people to remember. On the other hand, Joseph is thinking about changing his name to a less common name because he wants to be different and to be **unusual.**

People have a lot of reasons for changing their names. Movie stars, singers, and other entertainers often change their names because they want names that are **glamorous** and unusual or names that have a special sound. Like Anne, they often choose a name that is easy to say and to remember. Athletes sometimes change their names too. Here are some examples of name changes for some famous movie stars, singers, and athletes. The "new name" is the name they chose for themselves, and the "original name" is the name their parents gave them at birth.

New Name	Original Name
Muhammad Ali	Cassius Clay
David Bowie	David Jones
Cher	Cherilyn La Pierre
Sophia Loren	Sophia Scicoloni

---

[3] **"If I were Latino, José would be too common."** José ("Joseph" in Spanish) is a very common first name for Latino boys and men, but it is not common for Americans from other backgrounds (such as Korean-Americans and Japanese-Americans).

Walter Matthau	Walter Matuschanskayasky
Marilyn Monroe	Norma Jean Baker
Ringo Starr	Richard Starkey
John Wayne	Marion Michael Morrison
Raquel Welch	Raquel Tejaca
Stevie Wonder	Steveland Morris Hardaway

Some people change their names for religious reasons. For example, when the boxer Cassius Clay became a Muslim, he changed his name from Cassius Clay to Muhammad Ali to show the world that he was a new person because of his religious conversion. The head of the Roman Catholic Church, the pope, changes his name when he becomes pope. He takes the name of an **admired** religious person from the past, and he no longer uses a family name. For example:

Pope John Paul II

Another reason that some people change their names is that they have immigrated to a new country and want to use a name that is common in their new country. For example, Leung Kei Ming changed his name to Ken Leung when he immigrated to the United States. He uses the name Ken at his job and at school. But with his family and Chinese friends, he uses his original name. Did he really change his name? No, because he continues to use his original name in certain situations. But he added a new name for other situations. Using different names in different situations is common among immigrants, and, for some people, it makes life easier in their new country.

Sometimes people who have **broken the law** may use a different name to try to hide from the police and other authorities. A criminal may use several different names to try to avoid being captured.

In many countries, the family name of a woman changes to the family name of her husband after the wedding. But today, many women are keeping their own family name (their "maiden name") and not using their husband's name. Occasionally, women use their maiden name in some situations (at work, for example) and their husband's name in other situations. And some use both their maiden name and their husband's name. For example, when Hillary Rodham married Bill Clinton, she changed her name to Hillary Rodham Clinton.

Popular Names

In the United States, there are **fashions** in names, and these fashions change as time goes by, just as hairstyles and clothing fashions change. Names that were popular at one time may be out of fashion thirty or forty years later. This is especially true of girls' names. Let's look at girls' names that were popular in 1948 and in 1991:

1948	1991
1. Linda	1. Jessica
2. Mary	2. Ashley
3. Barbara	3. Amanda
4. Patricia	4. Jennifer
5. Susan	5. Sarah, Sara
6. Cathleen, Kathleen	6. Stephanie
7. Carol	7. Nicole
8. Nancy	8. Brittany
9. Margaret	9. Heather
10. Diane	10. Melissa

From these lists, we can see that the ten most popular names in 1948 are not the same as the ten most popular names in 1991.

Now let's look at the popular boys' names in these same years:

1948	1991
1. Robert	1. Michael
2. John	2. Christopher
3. James	3. Matthew
4. Michael	4. David
5. William	5. Daniel
6. Richard	6. Joshua
7. Joseph	7. Andrew
8. Thomas	8. James
9. Stephen	9. Robert
10. David	10. Ryan

We can see that the fashions in boys' names have not changed as much as the fashions in girls' names, although there have been some changes.

Can you guess the most popular names in England seven hundred years ago? Here they are:

Boys	Girls
William	Alice
John	Joan
Richard	Berthe
Robert	Blanche
	Beatrice

More than fifty percent of the males (men and boys) in England in 1295 A.D. had these names. There were only twenty-eight other male names in use at that time, according to historical records. The females (women and girls) in 1295 A.D. used more names than the males did, but they too did not use many different names. It is interesting to see that the boys' names from 1295 are still popular today. The girls' names from 1295 are still used, but they are not popular in today's world.

(871 words)

Second Reading: Filling in the Gaps

Read the passage a second time to help you understand it better. After you finish the second reading, work with another student in your class and try to guess the meanings of new words.

Third Reading: Putting the Information Together

Read the passage a third time as quickly as you can. Try to understand the meaning of the new words in their context as you read. Reading the passage a third time will help you understand the ideas and learn new vocabulary at the same time.

1. Understanding Ideas and Vocabulary

Draw a circle around the letter of the best answer. Talk about your answers with your classmates.

1. Which ones are entertainers?

    a.   Doctors, lawyers, accountants
    b.   Movie actors, singers, dancers
    c.   Clerks, typists, secretaries

2. Choose **two** reasons that an actress might change her name.

    a.   She wants a name that is quite unusual and hard to remember.
    b.   She wants a name that has a glamorous sound to it.
    c.   She wants a name that people will remember easily.

3. What is the main reason criminals might change their names?

    a.   To have names people will easily remember.
    b.   To avoid the police.
    c.   To have more popular, glamorous names.

4. Fashions in girls' names seem to change _____ fashions in boys' names.

    a.   more than
    b.   less than
    c.   about the same as

5. Match these words. Draw a line from the words on the left to the words on the right that mean almost the same thing.

    1. professional name   a.   the name given at birth
    2. a common name   b.   the name a person uses in his or her work
    3. traditional name   c.   a name that has been used for a long time in a culture
    4. original name   d.   a name that many people have
    5. maiden name   e.   a woman's original family name (before marriage)

2. Let's Talk!

These questions ask you about reasons that people may change their names in your culture. Talk about your answers with two or three of your classmates. After you finish talking, write your answers on the blank lines.

1. What are some of the reasons that people in your culture change their names?

    _____

    _____

    _____

2. Have you ever changed your name? If yes, what was your original

    name? _____

    What is your new name? _____

    Why did you change your name? _____

    _____

    How did you choose your new name? _____

    _____

3. Can you think of a famous (well-known) person who changed his

    or her name? _____

    _____

    Why do you think this person did so?

    _____

    _____

3.　The Name Game

Find these given names and draw a circle around each one: *Al, Alan, Amy, Ana, Ann, Anne, Ari, Eli, Hal, Ike, Jan, Jane, Jean, Jim, Jo, John, José, Lee, Maria, Mike, Naji, Ria, Sam*. Work as fast as you can. After you finish, talk with others in your group about the names you found.

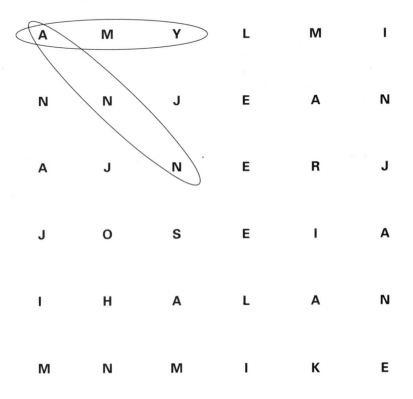

E X P A N S I O N   A C T I V I T I E S

Interview: Names and Naming Customs

You have discussed the naming customs of your culture in the "Let's Talk!" exercises above. Now interview a classmate about the naming customs in his or her culture. If possible, try to choose someone who comes from a different background than you do. First, read this sample interview so you can see how to conduct an interview. Marta is the interviewer, and she is asking Po Kwun about her name and the naming customs in her culture.

Marta: May I ask you some questions about your name, Po Kwun?

Po Kwun: Yes, I will be happy to answer.

Marta: Thank you. First of all, what is your full name?

Po Kwun: Shin Po Kwun.

Marta: What is your family name, and what are your given names?

Po Kwun: Shin is my family name, and my given names are Po and Kwun. All my sisters have the name Po, and then we each have a different given name after Po.

Marta: How interesting! So what are the names of your sisters?

Po Kwun: Po Ling, Po Ping, Po Mah, Po Lok, and Po Fun. By the way, Po means good or nice.

Marta: What about Kwun? Does it have a meaning too?

Po Kwun: Yes, it means "evergreen tree," a tree that stays green all winter and can **survive** in very cold weather.

Marta: Who named you?

Po Kwun: My father.

Marta: Why did he give you this name?

Po Kwun: He named me Po because he wanted me to be a good person. And he named me Kwun because he wants me to be strong in all situations—like the evergreen tree.

Marta: That's very interesting. Do you ever think about the meaning of your name?

Po Kwun: Yes, sometimes. I like my name very much because I want to be a strong, good person.

Marta: Po Kwun, you also chose an American name when you immigrated to the United States. What is your American name?

Po Kwun: Eva. I use this name at work because it's easier for Americans to say. Po Kwun is too unusual for them.

Marta: How do you feel about your new name?

Po Kwun: I like it. It makes me feel American.

Marta: Which name do you like better, Eva or Po Kwun?

Po Kwun: Oh, Po Kwun, **definitely**. Po Kwun is my true name, my real name. I use it with my family and my Chinese friends. But now I am an American too. Sometimes I am Eva—and sometimes I am Po Kwun.

Marta: Do you like having two names?

Po Kwun: Yes, because I like being Chinese, and I like being American too.

Marta: Thank you very much, Po Kwun. Or should I call you Eva?

Po Kwun: Oh, I don't care. Po Kwun or Eva, it's up to you.

Planning and Conducting the Interview

A. Plan your interview. Before you interview the person, think about the questions you want to ask. Write out these questions on a piece of paper. You may want to begin with the questions that follow. You can get ideas for other questions from Marta's interview with Po Kwun. Be sure to leave space on your paper for the answers.

1. May I ask you some questions about your name? _____

2. What is your full name? _____

3. What is your family name? _____

4. Is that your mother's family name or your father's? _____

5. Does your family name have a special meaning? _____

   _____

6. What is your given name? _____

7. Do you have more than one given name? _____

8. Who named you? _____

9. Why did this person give you this name? _____

10. Do you like your name? Does it have a special meaning?

   _____

   _____

Be sure to add other questions you would like to ask in your interview.

B.   Choose a classmate to interview.

C.   Begin your interview.   Do not try to write complete answers to your questions. Just make notes (write a few words) to help you remember the answers.

Interaction

Work with two or three other classmates. Tell the group about your interview. Tell them the name of the person you interviewed, and then tell them your questions and the answers that the person gave. Be sure to use your notes to help you remember what the person said in the interview.

Special Reading

This passage comes from a book written by Sandra Cisneros called *The House on Mango Street* (New York: Vintage Books, 1989). The main character of the book is a young Mexican-American girl named Esperanza, and in this passage she is talking about her name, what it means, and how she feels about it. (Reprinted by permission.)

My Name

In English my name means hope. In Spanish it means too many letters. It means sadness, it means waiting. It is like the number nine. A muddy color. It is the Mexican records my father plays on Sunday mornings when he is shaving, songs like **sobbing.**

It was my great-grandmother's name and now it is mine. She was a horse woman too, born like me in the Chinese year of the horse—which is supposed to be bad luck if you're born female—but I think this is a Chinese **lie** because the Chinese, like the Mexicans, don't like their women strong.

My great-grandmother. I would've liked to have known her, a wild horse of a woman, so wild she wouldn't marry. Until my great-grandfather threw a **sack** over her head and carried her off. Just like that, as if she were a **fancy chandelier.** That's the way he did it.

And the story goes she never forgave him. She looked out the window her whole life, the way so many women sit their sadness on an elbow. I wonder if she made the best with what she got or was she sorry because she couldn't be all the things she wanted to be. Esperanza. I have inherited her name, but I don't want to **inherit** her place by the window.

At school they say my name funny as if the **syllables** were made out of tin and hurt the **roof** of your mouth. But in Spanish my name is made out of a softer something, like silver, not quite as **thick** as my sister's name—Magdalena—which is **uglier** than mine. Magdalena who at least can come home and become Nenny. But I am always Esperanza.

I would like to baptize myself under a new name, a name more like the real me, the one nobody sees. Esperanza as Lisandra or Maritza or Zeze the X. Yes. Something like Zeze the X will do.
(331 words)

Freewriting

Write your name on a piece of paper, and then write for 15 minutes about your name. Write anything that comes into your mind—what your name means, who gave you this name, why you were given this name, if you were named after someone, and so on. Write about your feelings about your name. Do you like your name? Would you like to change it? Why or why not? What name would you choose?

After you finish, read your writing to some of your classmates, and listen to their writings about their names. Talk about the interesting points in each of the writings, and ask questions if you don't understand or if you would like to know more about something.

Quotation

Read this quotation and explain what it means:

"What's in a name? That which we call a rose
By any other name would smell as sweet."

WILLIAM SHAKESPEARE,
Romeo and Juliet, Act II, Scene ii

Cities

Before You Begin

DISCUSS THESE QUESTIONS WITH YOUR CLASSMATES:

1. Do you live in a city?
2. If so, do you like it?
3. What do you like about it?
4. What don't you like?
5. What is the most important city in your country?
6. Is it the largest city in your country?
7. Is it the **capital** (the center of government)?

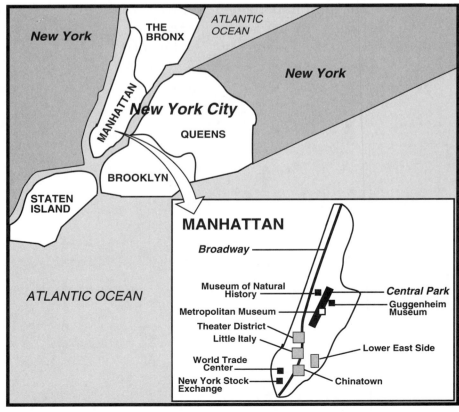

C H A P T E R   O N E

New York

In Unit 1, Joanna Medina was applying for a passport. Now she has just arrived at Kennedy Airport in New York, and she is going through U.S. Customs. She is talking to a **customs agent**. **Read this dialogue with a partner.**

Agent: Hello. May I see your passport, please?

Joanna: Yes, here it is.

Agent: You're Joanna Marisol Medina?

Joanna: Yes.

Agent: Why are you coming to New York?

Joanna: Just to visit. I'm on vacation for three weeks.

Agent: What is your address here?

Joanna: Do you mean here in New York?

Agent: Yes. Where will you be staying in New York?

Joanna: With my sister, Daniela Medina, in Brooklyn at 172 9th Avenue.

Agent: You're a **tourist** here? How long will you be here?

Joanna: Three weeks. Twenty days, as a matter of fact.

Agent: All right [**stamping** the passport]. Everything is in order. Have a good time. Enjoy your stay in the Big Apple!

Joanna: The big apple? What do you mean?A

First Reading: Getting the Main Idea

Read through the following passage. Try to understand the meaning, and don't stop to look up new words. Take as much time as you need to complete your first reading.

Bright Lights, Big City

New York City is the **largest** city in the United States. It is in New York state, and it has a **population** of more than seven million (7,000,000) people. Since the 1920s, people have called New York "The Big Apple." Entertainers, musicians, and **athletes** all wanted to perform in New York City, and they used to say, "There are many apples on the tree, but when you pick New York City, you pick The Big Apple." That's how it got the name.

New York City has five parts: Manhattan, Brooklyn, Queens, Staten Island, and the Bronx. These parts are the five **boroughs** of New York. Manhattan, Brooklyn, Queens, and Staten Island are all on islands. The Bronx is part of the **mainland.**

Manhattan is the city's **commercial** center. It is a very small **area**—only about 28 **square** miles—but it is the center of much of the **wealth** and **power** in the United States. It has some of the tallest buildings in the world, which are called **"skyscrapers"** because they reach up and touch, or "scrape," the sky. The twin towers of the World Trade Center are the tallest buildings in Manhattan. They were built in 1971, and they are 110 **stories** high (1,349 feet or 411 meters). When they were first built, they were the tallest buildings in the world, but in 1973 the Sears Tower in Chicago was built. The Sears Tower is 1,454 feet (443 meters) tall, so it is now the tallest building in the world.

Where to Go and What to Do in New York

"What can I do in New York?" It **depends** on how much time and money you have! No matter how long you are in New York, you can never see and do everything. There are more than 200 museums in New York City. Some of the most **famous** ones are the Metropolitan Museum of Art, the Museum of Modern Art, the Guggenheim Museum, and the Natural History Museum. New York is also the home of Broadway, the theater **district**, where there are hundreds of large and small theaters with plays for every **taste.** It's the home of Lincoln Center, where you can see operas and ballets and listen to all kinds of music. If you like sports, you can see **professional** baseball, basketball, ice hockey, tennis, and so on. New York has something to **offer** everyone.

If you are interested in **finance** and business, you can visit one of the **stock exchanges** in the financial district in lower Manhattan and see stocks and bonds being bought and sold. No matter what kind of food you like, you can find it in New York. There are thousands of restaurants that serve **specialities** from all over the world—for example, Chinese, Indian, Italian, French, Japanese, Brazilian, and Arabic. And if you like fashion, you can find any style you want in New York, no matter where it comes from. People often say, "If you can't get it in New York, it doesn't **exist.**"

The People

What are New Yorkers like? First of all, there is no **typical** or **average** New Yorker. They come in all colors, shapes, and sizes because they come from countries all over the world. English, of course, is the main language in New York, but you often hear Spanish, French, Russian, Chinese, Arabic, and many other

Chinatown, New York City

languages in the city. It is very **useful** to know more than one language in New York.

New York is truly a city of immigrants, and they bring their languages, traditions, and customs with them. In less than an hour, you can walk from Chinatown to Little Italy and then to Orchard Street, which is a street full of Jewish shops on the Lower East Side. You can continue on to East Sixth Street, a street full of Indian shops and restaurants. Without spending a penny or taking a ship or a plane, you can enjoy the experience of moving from one culture to another completely different one in just minutes. This is just one of the many interesting and **unusual** things that people like about New York.

Why do so many immigrants come here? Two important reasons are economic and educational opportunities. They want to get good jobs so they can make a better life for themselves and their children. They come to New York for educational opportunities, also. In addition to the elementary schools and high schools, there are many **vocational** schools and colleges and universities in New York. Immigrants can study English along with other subjects, and they can often get **financial aid** from the government to help them pay for their education. New York is truly a city of opportunity.

Rich and Poor

It is true that New York has many people with a lot of money, and these wealthy people can **afford** beautiful houses and apartments. They often have **limousines** and **chauffeurs** to drive them wherever they want to go. They can afford to buy the finest and most **expensive** clothing and go to the best restaurants, nightclubs, and theaters. They can buy whatever they want because they can afford to pay for it.

Unfortunately, New York is not a city of opportunity for everyone. There are also many people in New York who have very little or no money. Many of them live in poor, **run-down** apartments in **dangerous** areas full of **crime**. Some people do not have any place to live, and these **homeless** people live in the streets. They often sleep in the subway and train stations and in the public parks. People visiting New York for the first time are often **surprised** to see so many very rich people and so many very poor people living in the same city. The good and the bad, the **best** and the **worst**—you can find it all in New York.
(988 words)

Second Reading: Filling in the Gaps

Read the passage a second time to help you understand it better. After you finish the second reading, work with another student in your class and try to guess the meanings of new words.

Third Reading: Putting the Information Together

Read the passage a third time as quickly as you can. Try to understand the meaning of the new words in their context as you read. Reading the passage a third time will help you understand the ideas and learn new vocabulary at the same time.

1. Understanding Ideas and Vocabulary

Draw a circle around the letter of the **best** answer. Talk about your answers with your classmates.

1. The Big Apple is another name for

   a. New York City.
   b. people who live in New York City.
   c. New York state.

2. Which of the five boroughs of New York City are on islands?

   a. Brooklyn, Staten Island, Manhattan, the Bronx
   b. Brooklyn, Queens, Staten Island, the Bronx
   c. Brooklyn, Queens, Staten Island, Manhattan

3. Match these numbers. Draw a line from the numeral on the left to the correct number on the right.

   1. 7,000,000   a. seven hundred
   2. 7,000   b. seven million
   3. 700   c. seven
   4. 7   d. seventy
   5. 70   e. seven thousand

4. The population of New York City is _____ eight million.

   a.   exactly
   b.   less than
   c.   more than

5. Some of these statements are true, and some of them are not true. Read each statement carefully. Write **true** or **false** in each blank.

   _____ a.   New York is the largest city in the United States.

   _____ b.   New York has more than ten million (10,000,000) people.

   _____ c.   The Twin Towers of the World Trade Center are taller than the Sears building in Chicago.

   _____ d.   The five boroughs of New York are all on islands.

   _____ e.   Many people in New York come from other countries.

2. Let's Talk!

These questions ask you about the largest city in your country. Talk about your answers with two or three of your classmates. After you finish talking, write your answers on the blank lines.

1. What is the largest city in your country? _____

2. How big is this city? (How many people live in this city?)

   _____

   _____

3. What are some important things about this city?

   _____

   _____

   _____

4. What are some interesting things for people to see and do in this city?

_____

_____

_____

3. Vocabulary and Structure Practice

Choose the correct word and write it on the line. Talk about your answers with your group.

New York City is one of the largest _____ (1) in
cities—states—countries

the world. It is in the United States in the _____ (2) of
city—state—country

New York. New York City has five parts or _____ (3).
districts—areas—boroughs

Four of these five boroughs are on _____ (4)
land—the sea—islands

with water around them. Only the Bronx is not an island. More than

seven _____ (5) people live in New York. These
hundred—thousand—million

people come from all over the world. _____ (6) is the
Spanish—French—English

main language. But you hear many other _____ (7)
languages—radios—people

as well because immigrants _____ (8) their languages
brings—bring—brought

and customs with them. People usually come to New York

for _____ (9) and educational opportunities. They
economic—educational—fun

want to get good _____ (10). They also want good
houses—jobs—cars

lives for themselves and for their families. They want the

_____ (11) to go to school. There are many rich

car—opportunity—time

people in New York. But there are also many very poor people

_____ (12) money who _____ (13) not able to enjoy all

with—without   *is—are—were*

that New York has to offer. Even with all of its problems, New York

is a wonderful, _____ (14) city. There is no place in

exciting—excited

the world like the Big _____ (15)! Come and

Banana—Orange—Apple

see for yourself!

Beijing

L ook carefully at this map of the People's Republic of China before you begin reading.

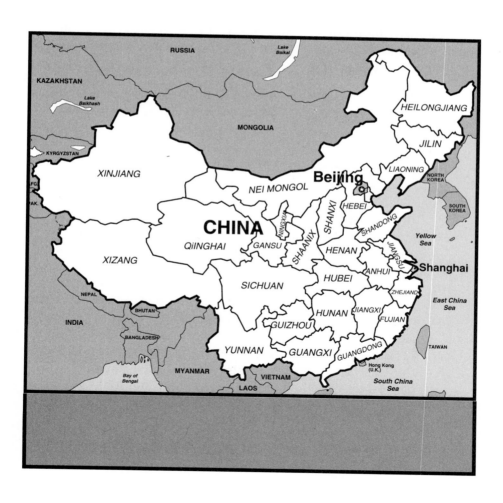

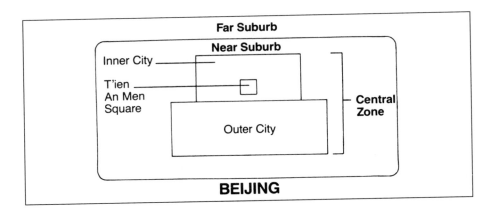

BEIJING

First Reading: Getting the Main Idea

Read through the following passage. Try to understand the meaning, and don't stop to look up new words. Take as much time as you need to complete your first reading.

Beijing: The Capital of the People's Republic of China

The capital of the People's Republic of China is Beijing (formerly called "Peking"). Beijing is not the largest city in China, but it is very important because it is the center of the Chinese government. It is also the cultural center of China and a center of industry and transportation. Shanghai is the largest city, and Beijing is the second largest.

Beijing is **located** in the northeast part of China. The city has mountains on three sides, and it is between the Yung-ting River and the Chai-pai River. This was an **excellent** place to build a city because it was safe. Before airplanes, enemies could not easily cross the mountains to get to Beijing, so it was a **secure** place. The rivers were important for transportation and for **trading** because they **connect** Beijing with other parts of China.

The city of Beijing covers a very large area: 9,500 square miles or 24,600 kilometers. You can compare its size to the country of Haiti or the state of New Hampshire in the United States.

The center of Beijing is the Central Zone, and it has two main parts: the Inner City and the Outer City. The Near Suburb and the Far Suburb surround the Central Zone.

T'ien An Men Square, Beijing

T'ien An Men Square

T'ien An Men Square is a very important place in the Inner City. It is a large, open area **surrounded** by the main government buildings and museums. The Great Hall of the People is on the west side of the square. The National People's Congress, the highest body of state power, meets there. It **elects** the government's leaders and makes decisions about the national economic plan. The Museum of Chinese History and the Museum of the Chinese Revolution are in a very large building on the east side of the square. In the middle of the square is the Monument to the People's Heroes, a monument for the great leaders of the country. The Mausoleum of Mao Zedong is on the south side of the square. Mao Zedong is **buried** there. He was one of the most important Communist leaders in China from 1949 to 1976, the year he died.

The Economy

Beijing is a modern manufacturing city, and it has many machine, chemical, and textile industries. It is also an important transportation center. Airplanes and trains connect Beijing with all parts of China and with cities all over the world. Beijing is an important city in the world today with great political power.

Communist Beijing

China has been a **communist** country since 1949. Although there are economic differences between people in Beijing, the differences are not as great as you find in western cities, such as New York and Mexico City. In other words, there are not as many very rich people and not as many very poor people in Beijing due to communism.

The economy of China has become stronger and more open since the late 1980s. Before that, there were **consumer shortages**, and it was difficult to find many things, especially **foreign merchandise**, in stores. Now the stores are full of merchandise, and you can buy things that come from all over the world. The Chinese economy is growing fast, and one of the problems that China may be facing now is that the economy may be growing too fast. This can cause **inflation**, which makes the cost of living very expensive because prices on everything go up very fast.

The People

The people and the way of living are special in every city in the world. One of the many things that tourists always find interesting and unusual in Beijing is the main transportation system. Everyone—old, young, man, woman—rides a bicycle. The streets are **crowded** with bicycles, especially during **rush hours** before and after work. Most of the cars are government cars or **taxis.** Not many people have private, family cars.

If you get up early in the morning in Beijing, you can see people doing their T'ai Ch'i exercises. People of all ages go outside to start their day off by doing their exercises. They say T'ai Ch'i is good for both the body and the mind.

In the past, everyone used to wear "Mao suits" to work and school. These blue or gray jackets and trousers and small caps were like **uniforms**, and they were made popular by Chairman Mao. However, most people today, especially young people, wear western-style clothing. You can see jeans and **miniskirts** and other international fashions on the streets of Beijing, although some older people still wear Mao suits.

The Problems of Change

As Chinese society became more open in the 1980s, people had new opportunities, but there were some problems too. People did not all agree on how much change and **openness** they wanted in their society. In 1989, students held **huge demonstrations** in T'ien An Men Square in Beijing to **demand** that the government give them more freedom and become more **democratic**. The government **responded** by sending in soldiers to stop the demonstrations. In the end, almost 4,000 people were killed in this **confrontation**. This was a **tragic** moment in recent Chinese history for everyone, no matter what their political ideas may have been at the time.

Housing in Beijing

Today, housing is a big problem in Beijing because there are not enough apartments for all the people who want to live there. The government is trying to build new apartments, but it cannot build fast enough to meet the **demand**. Many people want to live in Beijing because it is the capital city and because they may have family and friends there, but they cannot because of the **housing** shortage.

History

Beijing is a very, very old city although it has not always been called by the same name. A city with many other names has been in that location for more than 3,000 years. And 500,000 years ago, some of the first human beings were living in the area of Beijing, so the history of Beijing goes back a long time. **Historians, anthropologists,** and **archeologists** have always been interested in Beijing for this reason.
(1,000 words)

Second Reading: Filling in the Gaps

Read the passage a second time to help you understand it better. After you finish the second reading, work with another student in your class and try to guess the meanings of new words.

Third Reading: Putting the Information Together

Read the passage a third time as quickly as you can. Try to understand the meaning of the new words in their context as you read. Reading the passage a third time will help you understand the ideas and learn new vocabulary at the same time.

1. Understanding Ideas and Vocabulary

Write answers for the first two questions. Talk about your answers with your classmates.

1. What are the four main parts of Beijing?

   _____

   _____

   _____

2. What are some of the problems in Beijing today?

   _____

   _____

   _____

3. Match these words. Draw a line from the word(s) on the left to the words on the right that mean almost the same thing.

1.	bicycles	a. the meeting place of the National People's Congress
2.	a Mao suit	b. the main transportation in Beijing
3.	The Great Hall of the People	c. clothing people used to wear to work and school, now worn mainly by older people
4.	Mao Zedong	d. the kind of government in the People's Republic of China
5.	communist	e. chairman of the Chinese Communist Party from 1949 to 1976

4. Some of these statements are true, and some of them are not true.
   Read each statement carefully. Write **true** or **false** in each blank.

   _____ a.   Beijing is the capital of the People's Republic of China.

   _____ b.   Beijing is the largest city in China.

   _____ c.   Beijing is in the center of China.

   _____ d.   Beijing covers a very large area.

   _____ e.   Most people in Beijing today wear Mao suits.

5. Cross out the word that is **not** like the other two words. You may
   look up words in the glossary or in your dictionary.

   example: paper—pencil—st~~reet~~

   a.   northeast—country—south
   b.   the People's Congress—rivers—mountains
   c.   human beings—people—monkeys
   d.   culture—industry—manufacturing
   e.   old—modern—new

2. Let's Talk!

These questions ask you about the capital of your country. Talk about
your answers with two or three of your classmates. After you finish
talking, write your answers on the blank lines.

1. What is the capital of your country?

   _____

2. How big is the capital, and where is it located?

   _____

   _____

Is it the largest city in your country? _____ If it isn't, what is the

largest city? _____

3. Did you ever live in the capital? _____

If so, did you enjoy living there? Explain why or why not.

_____

_____

_____

_____

4. What are some interesting and unusual things about life in the
capital (or another city) in your country? What should a tourist try
to see or visit there?

_____

_____

_____

_____

5. What are some of the problems in your capital? Explain the
reasons for these problems, if you can.

_____

_____

_____

_____

_____

3. Vocabulary and Structure Practice

Choose the correct word and write it on the line. Talk about your answers with your group.

Beijing is the _____ (1) of the People's Republic of
city—capital—state

China but it is not the _____ (2) city in China. It is an
large—larger—largest

important center of culture, transportation _____ (3) industry.
and—or—but

Beijing _____ (4) in the northeast part of China.
is—was—will be

_____ (5) has mountains on three sides, and it is
She—He—It

_____ (6) two rivers, the Yung-ting River and
among—by—between

_____ (7) Chao-pai River. The main
a—an—the

_____ (8) in Beijing is the bicycle. The streets
architecture—place—transportation

are full of _____ (9) in the morning and evening
taxis—cars—bicycles

during rush hours. Beijing, like all other large cities,

_____ (10) some problems, and one of the most important
has—have—had

problems in the city today is _____ (11). Many people
people—food—housing

want to live in Beijing, but they cannot because

_____ (12) are not enough apartments for
they're—there—their

everyone who _____ (13) one.
want—wants—wanted

C H A P T E R   T H R E E

Mexico City

Look carefully at this map of Mexico before you begin reading.

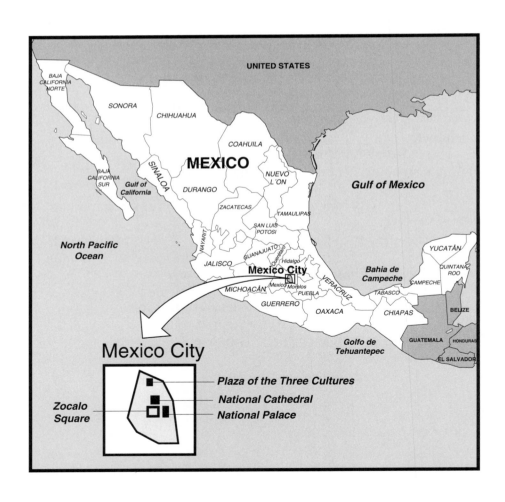

First Reading: Getting the Main Idea

Read through the following passage. Try to understand the meaning, and don't stop to look up new words. Take as much time as you need to complete your first reading.

Mexico City: One of the Largest Cities in the World

Mexico City (Ciudad de México) is the capital of Mexico. It is the largest city in Mexico and one of the largest cities in the world. It has a population of about 20 million (20,000,000) people. In the year 2000, the population will probably be more than 32 million (32,000,000).

Mexico City has an **unusual setting**. First of all, it has a very high **elevation**. It is 7,349 feet [2,240 meters] above sea level, and it is surrounded by mountains. It has a very pleasant, **temperate** climate with a temperature of about 70° F (21° C) in the hottest months and about 50° F (10° C) in the coldest months. It never gets **extremely** hot or extremely cold.

History

The Spaniards built Mexico City in 1521 at its present location. Before 1521, the Aztec city Tenochtitlan was at this location, and it was a very important city because it was the capital of the Aztec empire. Hernando Cortés, a Spanish leader, **invaded** the empire in 1519. He **conquered** the Aztecs and **destroyed** their great city. Since 1521, Mexico City has been the center for industry, commerce, and government. It is also the religious, cultural, and educational center of the country.

Places of Interest

The most important plaza or square in Mexico City is the Zocalo. This was also the governmental and religious center of the ancient Aztecs. The largest cathedral, the Metropolitan Cathedral, is located on the north side of the square. Christians built it partly of stone from the old Aztec temples that had been in the same location. On the east side of the square is the National Palace. This was the **site** of the palace of Montezuma, the last emperor of the Aztecs. On the west side of the Zocalo, there are many shops of various kinds.

Architecture in Mexico City

Mexico City is a **fascinating** city, partly because it is a **combination** of Aztec, colonial Spanish, and modern architecture. For example, the Plaza of Three Cultures has Aztec pyramids, a colonial church, and modern high-rise apartment buildings around it. In Mexico City, you get a strong feeling of the past and the present mixed together.

Culture

Mexico City is a major cultural center not only in Mexico, but in all of Latin America as well. It is the home of two symphony orchestras—the National Symphony and Mexico City Symphony—the National Opera Company, and the world-famous *Ballet Folklórico de México*. There are also many fine theaters throughout the city. Mexico City has always been **noted** for its artists and writers, many of whom are famous throughout the world.

Development

The Mexican economy has been growing fast in recent years. International companies as well as Mexican companies have been setting up **factories** and industries in Mexico and making products that are sold around the world. Many of these companies have their headquarters in Mexico City, so the city has become an international business center.

Development always brings opportunities and **challenges** together. An important challenge for the Mexican government is to figure out how to **protect** the **environment** and the rights of workers while it develops the economy. Every country faces this same challenge, but it is particularly important in Mexico now because the country is developing so fast.

The 1985 Earthquake

On September 19, 1985, there was a terrible tragedy in Mexico City that was **reported** around the world. An **earthquake struck** the city at 7:18 A.M. Thousands and thousands of people were on their way to work because it was rush hour. The earthquake lasted only four minutes, but in this short time, it completely destroyed more than 250 buildings in downtown Mexico City. It partially destroyed thousands of others. Apartment buildings, offices, and hospitals **collapsed**, and people died under **tons** of **rubble.** For days, **screams** and cries could be heard throughout Mexico City.

The next day, September 20, another earthquake hit Mexico City. This second quake was not as powerful as the first one. However, it destroyed many more buildings because they were

already **weakened** and **damaged** by the first quake. Worst of all, the second quake **injured** and killed even more people.

Two weeks after the earthquakes, **rescue** workers were still looking for people in the rubble. At that time, more than 7,000 people had been killed. Several thousand more were still missing, and some were never found. This **shocking** tragedy happened in just a few minutes. Many more people would have died, and only the long, hard work of thousands of rescue workers saved them. It will take a long time for Mexicans to forget the terrible tragedy of September 19–20, 1985. Many of them, especially those who lost **relatives** and **friends**, will never forget.
(794 words)

Second Reading: Filling in the Gaps

Read the passage a second time to help you understand it better. After you finish the second reading, work with another student in your class and try to guess the meanings of new words.

Third Reading: Putting the Information Together

Read the passage a third time as quickly as you can. Try to understand the meaning of the new words in their context as you read. Reading the passage a third time will help you understand the ideas and learn new vocabulary at the same time.

1. Understanding Ideas and Vocabulary

Choose or supply the correct answers. Talk about your answers with your classmates.

1. Mexico City was built by

  a. the Aztecs.
  b. the Spaniards.
  c. the Mexicans.

2. Mexico City is a combination of _____,

_____ , and _____ architecture.

3. Match these words. Draw a line from the word(s) on the left to the words on the right that mean almost the same thing.

1.   *Ciudad de México*   a.   the Spanish leader who conquered the Aztec empire

2.   7,349 feet   b.   Mexico City

3.   Tenochtitlan   c.   the last emperor of the Aztecs

4.   Hernando Cortés   d.   the elevation of Mexico City

5.   Montezuma   e.   the Aztec capital

4.   Some of these statements are true, and some of them are not true. Read each statement carefully. Write **true** or **false** in each blank.

_____ a.   Mexico City is the capital of Mexico.

_____ b.   Mexico City is larger than New York City.

_____ c.   Mexico City has a very low elevation.

_____ d.   Mexico City is extremely cold in the winter and extremely hot in the summer.

_____ e.   Mexico City is part of Latin America.

5.   Cross out the word that is **not** like the other two words. You may look up words in the glossary or in your dictionary.

a.   elevation—temperature—height
b.   happening—tragedy—disaster
c.   conquer—win—build
d.   hurricane—earthquake—rain
e.   temperature—climate—population

2. Let's Talk!

These questions ask you about the capital of your country. Talk about your answers with two or three of your classmates. After you finish talking, write your answers on the blank lines.

1. Hernando Cortés and the Spaniards built Mexico City in 1521. When was the capital of your country built? Who built it?

    _____

    _____

    _____

2. Mexico City has examples of Aztec, colonial Spanish, and modern architecture. What kinds of architecture are in the capital of your country? When were the oldest buildings built?

    _____

    _____

    _____

3. What do most of the buildings in your capital look like? What are the buildings made of? Wood, stone, brick? If possible, bring in pictures of the buildings in your capital. Show and explain them to the class.

    _____

    _____

    _____

    _____

4. Describe the climate in your country's capital. Is it a hot, temperate, or cold climate? Do you like the climate there? Why or why not? How does the climate affect the people who live there?

    _____

    _____

    _____

    _____

5. Who are some famous writers, musicians, or artists who have come from your country? When did they live? Why were they famous? What were some of their most famous works?

_____

_____

_____

_____

3. Vocabulary Practice: Word Forms

Read each sentence carefully. Then choose the correct word form from the list, and write it on the line. The first one has been done for you. (*Note:* This list has only the most common forms. It is not a complete list of all forms.) Talk about your answers with your group.

Word Form List

	Noun	Verb	Adjective	Adverb
1.	application applicant	to apply	—	—
2.	tradition	—	traditional	—
3.	connection	to connect	—	—
4.	interest	—	interesting	—
5.	entertainment entertainer	to entertain	entertaining	—

1. Please fill out this __*application*__ .

   What is the __*applicant*__ 's name?

   Do you want to __*apply*__ for a new passport?

2. What is your favorite holiday _____ ? Ernest is

   very _____ for someone so young.

3. Can you _____ this line with that one?

   I missed my _____ in Paris, and I had to wait nine hours for another plane.

4. Prague is a very _____ and beautiful city. It is located in the Czech Republic.

   Do you have an _____ in traveling?

5. Hollywood is part of the _____ industry.

   Who is your favorite _____ ?

   The singers will _____ the people for two hours.

   He is popular because he has a very _____ personality.

EXPANSION ACTIVITIES

Interview: Cities

You have discussed cities in your own culture in the "Let's Talk!" exercises above. Now interview a classmate about a city in his or her culture. If possible, try to choose someone who comes from a different background than you do.

Planning and Conducting the Interview

A. Plan your interview. Before you interview the person, think about the questions you want to ask. Write out these questions on a piece of paper. You may want to begin with the questions that follow. Then work with a partner to get ideas for more questions. Be sure to leave space on your paper for the answers.

1. May I ask you some questions about a city in your country?

    _____

2. What is the name of an important city in your country?

    _____

3. Why is it important? Is it the capital? _____

    _____

4. Is it the largest city? How big is it? _____

5. Does it have a good location? Describe it. _____

    _____

6. What about the climate? Does it have a good climate? Explain.

    _____

7. Tell me about the history. How old is the city? When was it built, and who built it?

    _____

    _____

8. What are some of the interesting places to visit and things to do in this city?

    _____

    _____

9. What are some other interesting things about this city?

    _____

    _____

Be sure to add other questions you would like to ask in your interview.

B. Choose a classmate to interview.

C. Begin your interview.   Do not try to write complete answers to your questions. Just make notes to help you remember the answers.

Interaction

Work with two or three other classmates. Tell the group about your interview. Tell them the name of the person you interviewed, and then tell them your questions and the answers that the person gave. Be sure to use your notes to help you remember what the person said in the interview.

Special Reading

This piece was written by Elsie Voltaire, a young woman who came to New York from Haiti.

Welcome to New York!

Everyone who comes to New York from another country for the first time has a story to tell. No matter where you are from or what you have experienced, your first day in New York is **bound** to be a big adventure, but this is especially true if you come from a small city or even a village on the other side of the world. Myself, I come from a small **provincial** city in Haiti, and I first arrived in New York on October 11, 1983.

There were so many airplanes arriving at the same time as mine. There was a sea of people moving in waves through the customs area into the main hall. I had never seen so many people and so many different kinds of people all speaking different languages. It was exciting, but I felt like a **tiny** drop of water in a big ocean. I could hardly wait to see my sister, who had sent me the airplane ticket and who was **supposed** to meet me at the airport.

I **searched** and searched for my sister in the big crowd of people waiting in the big hall. I couldn't find her. I waited and waited. No sister! Finally, I telephoned her home. No answer! Then I telephoned her office. I was so frightened because I could not speak English then, but I was able to make the secretary understand my sister's name. What a **relief!** My sister came to the telephone, and she explained that a big problem had **come up** at work and, **unfortunately**, she could not come to the airport to meet me. She told me not to worry, just to take a taxi to her house in Brooklyn and wait for her there.

"But I don't have the key!" I said. "How will I get inside?"

"Oh, don't worry. I left a key in the mailbox for you," she said. "Just go in and make yourself at home. Have something to eat, take a bath, have a nap and, before you know it, I'll be home. We'll go out to a restaurant for a nice dinner."

When the taxi driver got to my sister's street, he pulled over and stopped in front of a house that looked like all the other houses on the block. "Does my sister really live here?" I asked **nervously**, suddenly afraid to get out of the taxi.

"How should I know, lady?" he **snapped** at me. "I don't know every single person in New York City, you know." But then he was very nice, and he helped me carry the luggage up to the front porch. "Good luck!" he said, and he got back in his taxi and **zoomed off**. I was alone.

I looked at the house number, "135," and I started thinking maybe her house was "137"—or maybe "133." I was completely **confused**, and I suddenly realized I had left my address book at the airport in the telephone booth. What was I to do? I couldn't call my sister again because I didn't have her telephone number.

To make things worse, it was cold and gray, and it was just starting to rain. The New York weather seemed very cold and **forbidding** to me at that moment. As I was standing there looking up at the house number, I felt very far from my home and all alone in a strange land.

Then I remembered about the mailbox, and I cautiously looked inside. Thank goodness! The key was there, so this had to be her house! Why was I so silly to make all of these problems for myself! What a crazy imagination! I opened the door and took my things inside. At last, I felt safe and **at ease.** I was so **relieved** and exhausted from **anxiety** that I went to the bedroom and immediately lay down on the bed and took a nap. After perhaps a couple of hours, I woke up and had a soft drink and some chicken that was all prepared for me in the refrigerator. I even had a nice big piece of cake that was sitting on a pretty plate on the dining room table. I looked all around the house. What beautiful furniture and things my sister had!

Finally, I went into the living room and turned on the television. I watched a game show, *Wheel of Fortune,* but I couldn't understand a word. Night was falling, and I started wondering when my sister would arrive home from work. I looked out the window a few times—and suddenly I saw my dear sister walking down the sidewalk! I was so happy! I ran out the door and threw my arms around her and kissed her again and again. I did not want to ever let go of her!

"I didn't see you. Where did you come from?" she asked, laughing.

"From the house," I said. "I was in your house. I just came out when I saw you."

"My house?" she said. "What house?"

I looked at her, trying to **figure out** why she was **joking** with me. "Your house, of course!" I said and pointed at the open door behind me.

She looked up at the door, and then she looked at me, and then she looked back at the door. Her eyes opened wider and wider, and she didn't say a **single** word for a long time. Suddenly, she started laughing. She laughed so hard that tears were running down her face. Finally, she was able to tell me what was so funny. "That's not my house!" she said. "I live two houses down!"

I had gone into her neighbor's house. **By coincidence,** the neighbor had left her key in the mailbox also! I was so shocked and **horrified** at what I had done. All I could think about was cutting that big piece of cake from the pretty plate in the dining room. I was so **embarrassed.** Fortunately, the neighbor was a good friend of my sister's. Later on, we all had a good laugh about my mistake, and she became one of my best friends. We are **almost** like sisters, I could say!

I will never forget my first day in New York. Can you **blame** me?

(1,054 words)

Freewriting

Write your name on a piece of paper, and then write for 15 minutes about anything that comes into your mind related to this reading. You may wish to write about something that happened to you or someone you know.

After you finish, read your writing to some of your classmates, and listen to their writings. Talk about the interesting points in each of the writings, and ask questions if you don't understand or if you would like to know more about something.

Quotations

Read these quotations, and explain what they mean:

> **"The people are the city."**
>
> WILLIAM SHAKESPEARE,
> *Coriolanus,* Act III, scene i

> **"Fields and trees teach me nothing, but the people in a city do."**
>
> SOCRATES

Education

Before You Begin

DISCUSS THESE QUESTIONS WITH YOUR CLASSMATES:

1. Where did you go to school when you were a child?
2. How old were you when you started school?
3. Does everyone in your country have the opportunity to go to school?
4. How many years do most people in your country go to school?
5. Who pays for schools in your country?

Education in
the United States

In Unit 1, Anne Haddad and Joseph Lee met at a party. They are now talking about where they grew up and where they went to school. **Read this dialogue with a partner.**

Anne: Did you go to high school in Los Angeles, Joseph?

Joseph: Yeah, as a matter of fact, I went to Central High[1]. How about you?

Anne: Oh, my family is from Lebanon, and I went to a French school in Beirut when I was in elementary school, and then I went to school in France for three years. And after that, I came to the United States, and I went to high school in New York for a couple of years. And then we moved to California when I was ready for college.

Joseph: Your English is really good. Does your family speak English at home?

Anne: Sometimes. They speak Arabic and French most of the time at home though. I speak English most of the time now, I guess, except at home. How about you? Were you born here? You sound like a native Californian[2].

Joseph: No, I came when I was nine. I started in fourth grade. That was a terrible year for me because I didn't understand any English. I had a hard time until I was in junior high school when I was about 12. And then things got easier. You know, one day I just started thinking in English.

---

[1] **Central High** means Central High School. People often use this short form in conversation.
[2] **Native Californian** is a person who was born in California.

Anne: Your English is perfect now. You don't have any accent at all.
          I guess it's because you came here when you were so young.
          How's your Korean?

Joseph: Not so good. I sound like an American speaking Korean, my
          mother says. My grandmother came from Korea to live with
          us last year. She couldn't understand me at first. She asked
          my mother what was wrong with me! Now I'm teaching her
          English, and she's teaching me Korean. She's learning faster
          than I am, I think.

First Reading: Getting the Main Idea

Read through the following passage. Try to understand the meaning,
and don't stop to look up new words. Take as much time as you need to
complete your first reading.

Education and Values

People all around the world think education is important because
a good education usually means a better life. Everyone agrees with
that. However, schools are not the same in every country. This is
because people in different countries want their schools to teach
different things. Each culture has its own **values**, and people want
their schools to teach the values of their culture.

What do we mean by *values?* Values are people's ideas of the
best and most important ideas and beliefs in their culture. For
example, your culture may value hard work. That means that
people in your culture may respect hard work more than many
other qualities. Maybe religion is the most important value, or
perhaps art and creativity, or money and **material possessions.**

Some of the same values are important in different cultures.
However, there are many differences among cultural groups.
Within each culture, schools usually teach the values of that
culture, and children learn the values of their culture in school, as
well as at home.

The United States is a **democracy**, and democratic values are
very important. Everyone in the United States has the opportunity
to have free education. Local, state, and **federal** governments pay
for the public schools, and everyone, rich or poor, can go to
school. There are also many private schools. People in private
schools have to pay their own educational costs because the state
does not pay for private education.

Some people say that American schools try to do too much for too many people. They say it is impossible to give a good education to everyone. They think the American educational system should try to educate only the most intelligent people in the society **instead of** trying to educate everyone.

However, in a democracy, it is important for everyone to have an education because citizens in a democracy have to choose their government's leaders. They have to be able to understand ideas and issues clearly to make these choices, so they need a good education to be good citizens.

The Educational System in the United States

Elementary school: Most children in the United States start school when they are five years old. They go to kindergarten for a year and then start first grade when they are six. The first school is called elementary school, or grade school. American children learn to read and write when they are in first and second grade. They also begin to study **simple** arithmetic, science, and history, and in most schools, they have music and art lessons. In many schools now, even elementary school children learn how to use computers. They may play arithmetic games and write stories on the computer, or they may do a **group project**, such as **producing** a class newspaper once a week.

Junior high school or middle school: After elementary school, American children go to junior high school or middle school. In most school systems, junior high school includes seventh, eighth, and ninth grades, but sometimes it is only the seventh and eighth grades. Junior high school students are usually 12 to 14 years old. The main difference between a junior high school and a middle school is that middle school usually begins in fifth or sixth grade and goes through eighth grade. More and more schools are changing from the junior high school model to the middle school **model.**

High school: High school comes after junior high school or middle school. In the past, most high schools were **composed of** grades ten through twelve. In **recent** years, however, more and more high schools are composed of grades nine through twelve. Students usually graduate from high school when they are 17 or 18. There are different kinds of high schools to meet the special needs and interests of the students. Some high schools prepare students to go to college, and they are known as college-preparatory high schools. Other high schools prepare students for

A young volunteer hugs one of her buddies, an 89-year-old resident of a nursing home.

various kinds of work, and they are known as vocational high schools. Many high schools have both college-preparatory courses and vocational courses.

Some states are experimenting with **theme** high schools—for example, environmental studies, performing and visual arts (music, drama, dance, art), computer science, mathematics and science, and law. Theme schools allow students to **explore** their special interests and possibly decide on a career or profession to study in the future. For example, a student interested in law might go to a theme high school specializing in law. She would take a full **range** of courses, but part of the content of the courses would **relate to** law and law **enforcement** in society in some way. She would also probably work part-time in a law firm, in a court, or in a police station as part of her high school program. In this way, she could find out about the many different career opportunities in law, something about the **requirements** for these careers, and she could decide if she would enjoy going on to study more in a particular area after high school. On the other hand, if she discovered that she did not want to **pursue** a career in this area, she could change and study a different field in college.

More and more American high schools are trying to give students both academic courses and practical work experience at the same time. Many schools require students to do some sort of community service—for example, **tutoring** of younger children or, working in a library or a senior citizen center[3]. They usually do not get paid for this service, but they get some work experience and they make a **contribution** to their communities.

Higher education: When students graduate from high school, they may go on to a vocational school, college, or university. There are more than 3,000 colleges and universities in the United States. Some private colleges and universities are very expensive, but most state universities cost less. Financial aid (money from the government) and scholarships are often available to help students pay at least part of their tuition. Some form of higher education is **available** to every high school graduate.

Issues in American Education

Bilingual education: The United States is a country of immigrants who come from all over the world and speak many different languages. In the past, new immigrants had a hard time in American schools, and many of them became **discouraged** and **dropped out** of school because they could not understand their schoolwork in English. They were then not able to get good jobs because they didn't have a good education.

To help these new immigrants, many schools in the United States developed bilingual programs. (*Bi* means "two," and *lingual* means "language.") If a school had a lot of Spanish-speaking students, it might have a bilingual program where the Spanish-speaking students would study their subjects in both English and Spanish. A school with a large Chinese population might have an English-Chinese bilingual program. Students in bilingual programs are able to continue their general education and learn English at the same time. After a **period** of time when they have learned enough English, they can take all their classes in English with other students.

Bilingual education is **controversial**, meaning some people like it and are in favor of it, and other people are against it. The

---

[3] **Senior citizen center**—a community center with activities for older people. They may go there during the day to take classes, play games such as bridge or mah jong, and have lunch.

people in favor of bilingual education say, "It helps students to understand their schoolwork in history, mathematics, and science while they are learning English at the same time." These people say bilingual education helps students succeed in school, and the students can then get better jobs and be better citizens after graduation. Also, they **argue** that in the world today, it is a great **advantage** for people to know more than one language because they will have more professional and social opportunities. They say that all people should try to learn at least one other language in addition to their first language, and that in most countries around the world, people try to learn two or more languages well.

On the other hand, the people against bilingual education believe it is a **waste** of time and government money. They say that English is the main language in the United States and that everyone living in the United States should learn English as quickly as possible. They believe that bilingual education is too expensive and that the government should put bilingual education money into more programs to teach new immigrants English. Also, they **point out** that the government cannot afford to provide bilingual education for all immigrants because there are too many different languages, and it would be impossible to have a bilingual program for every language. Therefore, they say it is not fair to provide bilingual education for some immigrants and not for others.

The issue of bilingual education usually gets more attention when the economy is slow or not growing and the government does not have enough money to pay for all the programs that people want. Then people disagree about how the **limited** money should be spent. In conclusion, everyone has an opinion about bilingual education, but no one knows the best answer for sure because it is a very **complicated issue** with many sides to it.

National educational standards: In many countries around the world, all students at a certain level take a national exam in every course. They can then see how they compare with other students throughout the country at their grade level. Teachers can also look at their students' **results** and see how they are doing compared to other students. Although there are some problems with national exams, they help make the **standards** clear and fair for everyone.

In the United States, education is controlled by each state, instead of by the national or federal government. This means that education **varies** a great deal from state to state and even from school to school within a state. It is sometimes difficult to know how students from one school compare to students from another school because the standards may be completely different in the two schools.

People in the United States are talking about the need for national exams to help set standards. However, at the same time, states want to be able to control education within their state and to develop programs that meet the special needs of the people in their state. They do not want to be controlled by the federal government because they believe that educational policy that is good for one state may not be good for another state. Is it possible to have national exams and continue to have state control of education? This is a question that many people are discussing now because they want to make the American educational system better.

(1,825 words)

Second Reading: Filling in the Gaps

Read the passage a second time to help you understand it better. After you finish the second reading, work with another student in your class and try to guess the meanings of new words.

Third Reading: Putting the Information Together

Read the passage a third time as quickly as you can. Try to understand the meaning of the new words in their context as you read. Reading the passage a third time will help you understand the ideas and learn new vocabulary at the same time.

1. Understanding Ideas and Vocabulary

Choose or supply the correct answers. Talk about your answers with your classmates.

1. Most Americans believe that

    a. only the most intelligent people should have the opportunity to go to school.

    b. only the richest people should have the opportunity to go to school.

    c. everyone, rich or poor, intelligent or not so intelligent, should have the opportunity to go to school.

2. What is a theme high school?

    _____

    _____

3. Why do many schools require community service?

    _____

    _____

4. Match these words. Draw a line from the word(s) on the left to the words on the right that mean almost the same thing.

    1. kindergarten   a. the years between kindergarten and middle school or junior high school

    2. elementary school   b. the years after junior high or middle school

    3. middle or junior   c. the year before elementary school
        high school
    4. high school   d. the years between elementary and high school

    5. college or university   e. after high school

5. Some of these statements are true, and some of them are not true. Read each statement carefully. Write **true** or **false** in each blank.

    _____ a. All public and private schools in the United States are free.

    _____ b. Elementary school is the same thing as grade school.

    _____ c. Middle school is the same thing as high school.

    _____ d. The national or federal government controls education in the United States and tells each state what to do.

    _____ e. There are more than 3,000 colleges and universities in the United States.

2. Let's Talk!

These questions ask you about the educational system in your country. Talk about these questions with two or three of your classmates. After you finish talking, write your answers on the blank lines.

1. When do children start school in your country?

   _____

2. How many years are children in elementary school?

   _____

   Does your country have middle schools or junior high schools?

   _____

   How many years do students go to this school?

   _____

   How many years is high school in your country?

   _____

3. What subjects do children study in elementary school?

   _____

   How many hours do they go to school each day?

   _____

   What time does the school day begin, and what time does it end?

   _____

   How many days do children go to school each week?

   _____

   Which days do they go to school?

   _____

4. What are some interesting and unusual things about schools in your country?

_____

_____

3. Vocabulary and Structure Practice

Choose the correct word and write it on the line. Talk about your answers with your group.

People in _____ (1) countries around the world
                some—most—no

value education because _____ (2) believe that they
                        they—them—their

can _____ (3) a better life with _____ (4) good
    have—has—had   *a—an—the*

education. Also, in the United States people value

_____ (5) a great deal. They think it is very
money—life—education

_____ (6) for people _____ (7) a democracy to be
nice—important—well   *in—on—at*

able to _____ (8) intelligent decisions about
        made—have—make

_____ (9) government and laws of their society. The public
a—an—the

schools _____ (10) the United States _____ (11) free so
        in—on—at   *am—is—are*

everyone _____ (12) the opportunity to go to school. Most
         have—has—had

school systems _____ (13) six years of elementary school, three
               has—have—had

years _____ (14) junior high school _____ (15)
      with—of—in   *with—of—and*

three years of high school. In general, the United States has a

well-developed public education system.

Education in Saudi Arabia

L ook carefully at this map of the Middle East before you begin reading. Pay particular attention to Saudi Arabia.

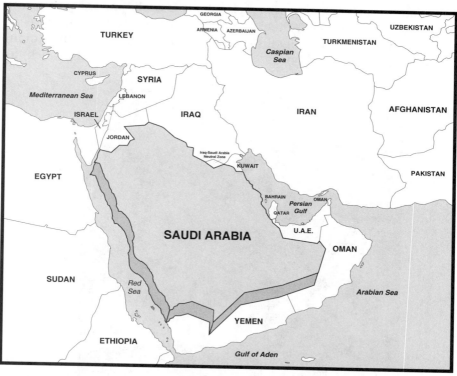

First Reading: Getting the Main Idea

Read through the following passage. Try to understand the meaning, and don't stop to look up new words. Take as much time as you need to complete your first reading.

Saudi Arabia

Saudi Arabia is a large Middle Eastern nation, about one-third the size of the United States and the same size as all of western

Europe. It is one of the world's biggest **producers** of oil. Saudi Arabia **exports** more oil than any other nation, and the money from this oil makes it a very rich country. Saudi Arabia has about 12 million people, and **virtually** all of these people are Arab Muslims. In other words, they are followers of the Islamic religion. Saudi Arabia is a religious nation. The king of Saudi Arabia is both the political leader and one of the religious leaders of the country. The government law is Islamic law (Muslim religious law), and the national language is Arabic.

The Islamic religion plays an important **role** in all aspects of Saudi Arabian society. For example, it is an important part of the Saudi educational system. Before 1950, almost all education in Saudi Arabia was religious education. Students studied the Koran, the Islamic holy book. They tried to **memorize** as much as

In Saudi Arabia, boys and girls do not attend the same schools after a certain age. Pictured above are gender-segregated classrooms.

possible from this book, and a well-educated person was someone who knew the Koran well. There were no colleges or universities before 1949 and only a few elementary and secondary schools.

In 1953, the Saudi government **established** the Ministry of Education. This was really the beginning of the modern educational system in Saudi Arabia. When engineers discovered oil in Saudi Arabia in the 1930s, the country suddenly started to become very wealthy, and Saudi leaders realized that Western technology was necessary for the country to develop both its oil resources and other industries. They still believed that religious education was very important, but they also believed that a modern country could not develop technologically with only a religious educational system. Therefore, they decided to add other subjects to their educational system. They wanted to combine traditional religious education with **modern technological** education from the West in a way that would be good for their culture and for the future development of their country.

Religion is still a very important part of Saudi education. Now, however, Saudi students study all kinds of other subjects too: languages (especially English), history, science, mathematics, computer technology, and so on. Before 1950, there were about 20,000 students in Saudi Arabia. In 1990, there were more than 2.5 million students. The educational system has grown faster in Saudi Arabia than in almost any other country in the world. The government gives full support to the schools. In other words, education is free at all levels, from elementary through university.

The Educational System in Saudi Arabia

Elementary school: Most children start school at the age of six, and they go to elementary school for six years. They study religion about one third of the time in elementary school. The rest of the time, they study general subjects.

Intermediate school: After elementary school, students go to intermediate school for three years. They can choose some of the subjects they want to study at this level. For example, they can choose science, history, or literature. Religion is a required subject for all students.

High school (secondary school):   High school lasts three years. Students can choose to go to an academic high school (college-preparatory high school) or a vocational school, where they learn a trade. Students in the academic high school can choose to study either a science program or a literature program. The science program is very popular, partly because it leads to the greatest number of educational and career opportunities later on. All students continue to study religion in high school.

Higher education: Higher education has grown **rapidly** in the last thirty years. In 1957, Saudi Arabia had only one college with just 25 students in it. However, by 1990 there were 78 colleges, including 11 women's colleges, and seven universities in Saudi Arabia—and more than 108,000 students! The Saudi government spent about $10.7 billion dollars on higher education between 1985 and 1990. It is trying to encourage as many people as possible to go to college and university because the country needs highly trained people to work in a variety of areas in the rapidly developing society. All colleges and universities are completely free. Additionally, the government gives money to students in colleges and universities to encourage them to go to school. A Saudi student may want to take special courses that are not **available** in any of the colleges and universities in Saudi Arabia. In that case, the government will send the student to another country to study, pay all expenses, and give the student a **stipend** (additional spending money) as well.

Career Opportunities in Saudi Arabia

Saudi Arabia is developing rapidly because of the wealth produced by oil. As a result of this development, there are many career opportunities for people with a good education. **Graduates** of a college or university can get a good position because there are so many jobs available in the society. However, even though the Saudi government does everything possible to encourage education, the country still does not have enough well-trained people to fill all the positions in industry and government. Therefore, the government invites many people from other countries to come to Saudi Arabia to work in all kinds of jobs in the society. In the future, the government hopes that they will have enough well-trained Saudis to be able to fill most, if not all, of these positions that are now held by **guest workers.**

Issues in Saudi Education

Segregated schools: In Saudi Arabia, the schools are **gender segregated.** This means that boys and girls (and later, men and women) do not go to the same schools. Some elementary schools have mixed classes (boys and girls in the same classes) in the lower grades. However, the schools are completely segregated after the first few years. This is because of the Islamic religion. According to Islamic tradition, girls after the age of nine or ten must not be with boys or men outside their own families.

The Saudi government decided that it wanted to offer educational opportunities for girls as well as boys, so the government started the first school for girls in 1956. At first, religious leaders did not like the idea of formal education for women because they **feared** it would have a bad **effect** on the family and the society. Therefore, to get the religious leaders to accept education for women, the government placed women's education under the direction and control of the country's religious leaders.

Women now attend women's colleges or special university departments for women. They have women teachers in the classroom. However, because there are not enough women teachers, the government allows men teachers to teach Saudi women through television. The women watch the **lectures** on television, and, they later can talk with the teacher on a special telephone to ask questions about the lecture. In this way, students and teachers never see each other face-to-face. This is an interesting example of how Saudi Arabia has used technology to **maintain** its cultural traditions.

Saudi women in a chemistry lab.

After graduation, Saudi women have many job opportunities, just as the men do. For example, they can work as teachers, doctors, social workers, and scientists. With very few **exceptions**, the **workplace** is also segregated. In other words, women and men do not work together except sometimes in hospitals. Saudi women want to have even more job opportunities than they have now, and, in particular, they would like to have more authority and decision-making responsibilities in their jobs. However, most of them say they do not **wish** to work with men. In a recent article in a magazine called *The Middle East,* some Saudi women students said, "We want good jobs and more professional opportunities, but we don't really want to work **alongside** men. We find many **positive points** in our system."
(1,321 words)

Second Reading: Filling in the Gaps

Read the passage a second time to help you understand it better. After you finish the second reading, work with another student in your class and try to guess the meanings of new words.

Third Reading: Putting the Information Together

Read the passage a third time as quickly as you can. Try to understand the meaning of the new words in their context as you read. Reading the passage a third time will help you understand the ideas and learn new vocabulary at the same time.

1. Understanding Ideas and Vocabulary

Choose or supply the correct answers. Talk about your answers with your classmates.

1. In the 1950s, Saudi Arabia changed its educational system. Saudi Arabia

    a. added religious courses.
    b. added modern, technological courses.
    c. dropped religious courses.

2. "Gender-segregated education" means that

   a. females and males attend the same classes.

   b. only males go to school.

   c. females and males go to different schools.

3. In your opinion, what are two interesting and important things about education in Saudi Arabia?

   _____

   _____

4. Match these words. Draw a line from the word(s) on the left to the words on the right that mean almost the same thing.

1.	educational stipend	a.	main source of Saudi Arabian wealth
2.	Saudi Arabia	b.	the Islamic holy book
3.	Arabic	c.	money given by the government to students to encourage them to go to school
4.	oil	d.	national language of Saudi Arabia
5.	the Koran	e.	large Middle Eastern nation

5. Cross out the word that is **not** like the other two words. You may look up words in the glossary or in your dictionary.

   a. decreasing—developing—growing

   b. oil—gas—water

   c. discovered—created—found

   d. socialism—Islam—Christianity

   e. mixed—segregated—combined

2. Let's Talk!

These questions ask you about aspects of education in your country. Talk about your answers with two or three of your classmates. After you finish talking, write your answers on the blank lines.

1. Religion is an important part of education in Saudi Arabia. Is religion important in the educational system in your country?

   _____ Explain and give examples.

   _____

   _____

   Do you think religion should be a required part of education? Why or why not?

   _____

2. In Saudi Arabia, the government strongly encourages young Saudis to go to school. It pays all educational expenses and gives students a stipend as well. Does the government in your country encourage people to go to school? Explain and give examples.

   _____

   _____

   _____

3. Women in Saudi Arabia have many educational and career opportunities. Do women in your country have the opportunity to get a good education? Explain and give examples.

   _____

   _____

   Does the government in your country encourage women to get a good education? If so, how does it encourage them?

   _____

   _____

   If not, why doesn't the government encourage them?

   _____

   _____

4. The schools in Saudi Arabia are gender segregated. Is this true in
    your country? _____ What do you think about gender-
    segregated schools?

    _____

    _____

    _____

5. What are some of the changes in education in your country in the
    last twenty or thirty years?

    _____

    _____

    _____

    _____

3. Vocabulary and Structure Practice

Choose the correct word and write it on the line. Talk about your
answers with your group.

Saudi Arabia is a(n) _____ (1) oil-producing country
                        large—small—old

in the Middle East. The citizens of Saudi Arabia _____ (2)
                                                   is—are—were

Muslims, and religion is _____ (3) important part of
                          a—an—the

life _____ (4) Saudi Arabia. Students _____ (5)
     for—in—by   *study—practice—do*

religion from elementary school through university. At the same

time, _____ (6) study other subjects such as literature,
      boys—they—can

science, and mathematics. Education is _____ (7)
                                        expensive—free—difficult

in Saudi Arabia, and the government _____ (8)

<u>encourages—forces—makes</u>

young Saudis to go to school. Saudi Arabia _____ (9)

<u>need—needed—needs</u>

well-educated and well-trained _____ (10) to help

<u>men—women—people</u>

develop _____ (11) country. Both women and men

<u>a—an—the</u>

_____ (12) educational opportunities in Saudi Arabia, but

<u>has—have—had</u>

the schools _____ (13) gender segregated. In other words,

<u>is—were—are</u>

males and females do not go to the _____ (14) schools.

<u>elementary—high—same</u>

Finally, Saudi Arabia combines traditional religious education with

_____ (15) technological education to try to meet the

<u>traditional—modern</u>

special needs and values of the society.

Education in South Korea

Look carefully at this map of the Pacific Rim before you begin reading. Pay particular attention to South Korea.

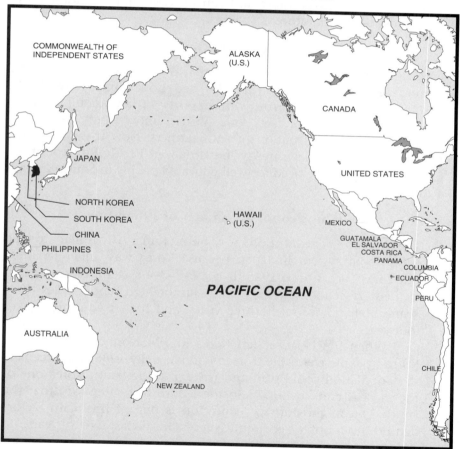

First Reading: Getting the Main Idea

Read through the following passage. Try to understand the meaning, and don't stop to look up new words. Take as much time as you need to complete your first reading.

The Pacific Rim

One of the fastest developing areas in the world today is the Pacific Rim region. This is a **huge region** going from the west coast of South America northward and across the Bering Strait to the **former** Soviet Union (USSR) and southward to Australia. The Pacific Rim **includes** all countries touched by the waters of the Pacific Ocean. Japan is the economic leader of the Pacific Rim today, but China and the "Four Tigers" (South Korea, Taiwan, Hong Kong, and Singapore) are all developing rapidly, and they are expected to **dominate** and control economic development in this region in the future.

South Korea's Rapidly Developing Economy

Countries such as South Korea that were extremely poor and undeveloped just a few **decades** ago now **compete** with the United States and Japan with **exports** of automobiles, ships, computers, television sets, and VCRs. Only twenty years ago, South Korea was a nation of poor farmers. Now it is one of the fastest growing of the newly industrialized Pacific Rim countries. Consequently, the need for well-educated people in South Korea is **extraordinary**.

The Economic Impact of Education

The system of education in South Korea is similar to the educational system in Japan because Korea was under Japanese rule for 35 years until 1945. It is a 6–3–3–4 system, meaning that elementary school takes six years, junior high school takes three years, high school takes three years, and higher education takes four years.

When the Japanese left Korea in 1945, only about half the Korean people were able to read and write. By 1986, 98 percent of the population could read and write, making South Korea one of the most **literate** countries in the world. It is often said that the South Korean **passion** for education is one of the main factors behind the country's economic success in the last twenty years.

Educational Problems and Successes

In South Korea, about 36 percent of high school graduates go on to higher education. This is an extremely high percentage for a newly industrialized country; it is a higher percentage than in France (30 percent), Italy (26 percent), Germany (18 percent), and

the Netherlands (15 percent), and it is comparable to the United States (44 percent) and Japan (39 percent).[4]

Higher education has great **value** in South Korea, and families do almost anything they can to give their children a chance for university education. Sometimes, they even move to be close to a high school with a high success rate on the university entrance exam.

Young people spend almost all their time in high school preparing for the final exam that will decide whether or not they can go on to university. One high school student described a typical school day this way: His school day begins every day at 7:30 a.m., goes on all day, and continues with special evening study classes until 10 p.m. Then he returns home and studies one more hour before going to bed. On Sundays, one of his parents stays home with him while he studies all day.

Why do students study so hard? What **motivates** them to give up everything for their studies? It is because there is great **competition** to get into universities and colleges. There are not nearly enough university places for all the people who want to go. In 1986 (a typical year), about 800,000 students took the national university entrance exam for only 250,000 places in colleges and

---

[4] Statistics comparing these countries are from the late 1980s. Percentages may be slightly different in the 1990s.

universities. In other words, 550,000 of these 800,000 students would not be successful in **fulfilling** their dream of a university degree even though they had studied night and day for years to prepare for this exam.

Student success in math and science: South Korean high school students do better than students from other countries around the world in international math and science exams. Their long study hours and preparation in test-taking skills clearly show positive results on **multiple-choice exams**. In high school, students take practice multiple-choice exams about twice a month. To prepare for these exams, they memorize a great deal of material (60–100 pages for each exam), and they get used to answering multiple-choice questions quickly and **accurately.**

Critics of the Educational System: However, many South Korean educators, parents, and students are very **critical** of their educational system. One **complaint** is that it puts too much **pressure** on young people, and high school students do not have time to do anything but study. Many people believe this is unhealthy because it does not allow young people to grow and develop as they should. As one teacher said, "**Adolescence** is a very important period in character development. This system only allows for a particular form of academic growth, leaving no time for anything else." Parents and students complain that the **pressure** is too great and the **workload** is too heavy. They point out that some students **commit suicide** each year because of the academic pressure and the **fear** of **failure**. One mother said, "The only time I see my children is when they are studying. They don't have time for anything else. They have no free time."

Educational Reform: Many South Korean educators want to **reform** the system because they believe it teaches students how to memorize but not how to reason and think **logically**. One South Korean university professor said that his students have trouble analyzing ideas and presenting their opinions: "They are lost if you ask them to do anything besides taking a multiple-choice test. They do not know how to think creatively and to solve problems. They do not know what they think about anything."

The South Korean government leaders are working on reforming the educational system. They want to change the **curriculum** in certain ways to give students from different areas and different schools an equal chance to succeed. But they admit that they do not have the financial **resources** to enlarge the

South Korean students have a great deal of pressure on them.

higher education system enough to meet the huge demand. In other words, they do not have enough money to create enough university places for everyone who wants to go. Consequently, the problem of extreme academic pressure on high school students will probably continue into the future.

Some Interesting Facts about South Korean Education: People in South Korea are certainly highly educated. Half of Seoul's adult population is either attending university or has already graduated. Furthermore, education doesn't stop with university. Many Korean companies provide on-the-job training for their employees so that they can learn new technology and applications of the technology. Another interesting fact: South Korea has the highest number of Ph.D.'s per capita.[5]

Finally, the South Korean educational system has an **outstanding record** of success, even though the system has some problems that many South Koreans would like to reform.
(1,190 words)

---

[5]**Ph.D's per capita**—number of people with doctorates (doctor of philosophy degrees) in the society. In other words, for its population size, South Korea has the highest number of people with the highest academic degrees.

Second Reading: Filling in the Gaps

Read the passage a second time to help you understand it better. After you finish the second reading, work with another student in your class and try to guess the meanings of new words.

Third Reading: Putting the Information Together

Read the passage a third time as quickly as you can. Try to understand the meaning of the new words in their context as you read. Reading the passage a third time will help you understand the ideas and learn new vocabulary at the same time.

1. Understanding Ideas and Vocabulary

Choose or supply the correct answers. Talk about your answers with your classmates.

1. South Korea is

    a.   one of the "Four Tigers."
    b.   a Pacific Rim country.
    c.   both of the above.

2. According to this passage, South Korea has more students going on for higher education than

    a.   Germany, France, Italy, and Japan.
    b.   France, Italy, the United States, and the Netherlands.
    c.   Germany, France, Italy, and the Netherlands.

3. Match these words. Draw a line from the word(s) on the left to the words on the right that mean almost the same thing.

1.	Seoul	a.	the present economic leader in Asia
2.	"The Four Tigers"	b.	all countries, states, and territories in and around the Pacific Ocean
3.	The Pacific Rim	c.	Taiwan, Singapore, Hong Kong, and South Korea
4.	Japan	d.	the capital of South Korea

4. Some of these statements are true, and some of them are not true. Read each statement carefully. Write **true** or **false** in each blank.

_____ a. South Korea has a high rate of illiteracy.

_____ b. High school students have a great deal of academic pressure on them.

_____ c. Most high school students who apply to university are accepted.

_____ d. People in Seoul, the capital of South Korea, tend to be highly educated.

_____ e. Korean companies do a lot of on-the-job training for their employees.

5. Cross out the word or phrase that is **not** like the other two words or phrases. You may look up words in the glossary or in your dictionary.

a. illiterate—literate—able to read and write
b. include—leave out—be part of
c. unusual—typical—average
d. fulfill—achieve—fail
e. workers—employers—employees

2. Let's Talk!

These questions ask you about education in your country and in the countries you have just read about. Talk about your answers with two or three of your classmates. After you finish talking, write your answers on the blank lines.

1. What was the most interesting part of this passage for you?

   Explain why it was interesting. _____

   _____

   _____

   _____

   _____

2. South Korean high school students have a great deal of pressure on them because it is so difficult to get into a university. Do students in your country have this kind of pressure on them? If so, explain why.

_____

_____

_____

_____

3. Describe a typical school day for a high school student in your country.

_____

_____

_____

Do high school students in your country work as hard as South Korean high school students do? Explain.

_____

_____

_____

4. Compare the educational systems of the United States, Saudi Arabia, and South Korea. In your opinion, what is the best point about each system?

_____

_____

_____

_____

_____

3. Vocabulary Practice: Word Forms

Read each sentence carefully. Then choose the correct word form from the list, and write it on the line. (*Note*: This list has only the most common forms. It is not a complete list of all forms.) Talk about your answers with your group. **Be careful with singular/plural forms of nouns.**

Word Form List

	Noun	Verb	Adjective	Adverb
1.	education educator	to educate	educational	—
2.	difference	to differ	different	differently
3.	requirement	to require	required	—
4.	experiment	to experiment	experimental	
5.	decision	to decide	decisive	—

1. This unit is about _____ in the United States, Saudi Arabia, and South Korea.

   What do you think of the _____ system in your country?

   Does your country try to _____ everyone?

   _____ don't always agree on educational policy.
   (*Hint*: Use plural here.)

2. We _____ in our opinions on what is important to learn.

   Is there any _____ between these two schools?

   My friend and I didn't learn the same things because we were in

   _____ classes.

   We don't have the same ideas because we look at the world

   _____.

3. Is religion a _____ course in your school?

    What are the school _____ for graduation?

    They _____ students to study science every year.

4. I want to study chemistry because I like to conduct scientific

    _____.

    The laboratory cannot _____ with human beings
    because it might be too dangerous.

    This is an _____ drug, so you cannot buy it in a
    pharmacy.

5. Camilla cannot _____ what she would like to

    study. She is trying to be very careful because it is an

    important _____.

    She will not have a problem because she is usually a very

    _____ person and knows what she wants.

E X P A N S I O N   A C T I V I T I E S

Interview: Education

You have discussed education in your own culture in the "Let's Talk!" exercises above. Now interview a classmate about the educational system in his or her culture. If possible, try to choose someone who comes from a different background than you do.

Planning and Conducting the Interview

A. Plan Your Interview.   Before you interview the person, think about the questions you want to ask. Write out these questions on a piece of paper. You may want to begin with the questions that follow. Then work with a partner to get ideas for more questions. Be sure to leave space on your paper for the answers.

1.   May I ask you some questions about the educational system in your country?

2.   At what age do children begin school in your country? _____

     What is this school called, and how long do children attend it?

     _____

3.   What subjects do children study in elementary school?

     _____

     How many days a week do they go to school? _____

     How many hours a day do they go to school? _____

     Is elementary school free for all students? _____

     Do all children in your country go to elementary school? _____

     Is this required by law? _____

4. (Here, make up some questions about junior high school and high school.)

5. (Here, make up some questions about higher education.)

6. (Suggestion: Ask some questions about academic pressure on high school students, how hard they have to study to get into university, or, perhaps, ask what a typical school day is for a high school student.)

7. (Suggestion: Ask about the good points in the educational system.)

8. (Suggestion: Ask about the things that need to be changed in the system because they are problems.)

9. (Suggestion: Ask about other interesting things in the educational system.)

Be sure to add other questions you would like to ask in your interview.

B.   Choose a classmate to interview.

C.   Begin your interview.   Do not try to write complete answers to your questions. Just make notes to help you remember the answers.

Interaction

Work with two or three other classmates. Tell the group about your interview. Tell them the name of the person you interviewed, and then tell them your questions and the answers that the person gave. Be sure to use your notes to help you remember what the person said in the interview.

Special Reading

This reading comes from a book titled *Iron & Silk,* by Mark Salzman (New York: Vintage Books, 1986). Mr. Salzman, a young American, went to China to teach English at Hunan Medical College in Changsha from 1982 to 1984 and to study kung-fu (martial arts). Some of his students at the college were known as the Middle-Aged English Teachers. In this passage, Mark Salzman is talking about the day these teachers read aloud to the class their compositions about their happiest moment.

After our ten-minute break for tea between the two hours, I decided to put away the textbook and ask them to read aloud their latest compositions, entitled "My Happiest Moment." They all thought this was a very good idea, but no one wanted to read first. Finally I called on Teacher Xu. He **shrugged** his shoulders with **resignation** and began.

"My happiest moment. When I was a young man I attended a dance at night. We were all very excited about this dance. The music was being played, and stars shone brightly. I saw a girl standing, and wanted to ask her to dance, but as I am shy and full of fear, I did not **dare**! But then I did, and we danced. I did not know her name. We did not talk, we only danced. We danced in circles, around and around, and the stars went around and around, and my cheek touched hers. The room disappeared, the other people disappeared, and I could only see the stars dancing around and around. After that, I did not see her ever again. I wonder where she is."

The rest of the class **clicked** their tongues in **mock** disapproval of his romantic story and **teased** him, asking if he had shown this essay to his wife. Teacher Xu smiled faintly, shrugged again and said, "She cannot read English."

Next I called on Teacher Zhang. . . . At first he **declined** to read; sitting sideways in his chair and shaking his head, he said he was a sad man and could not remember a happy moment. But his **colleagues** insisted that he had written an essay and **coaxed** him into reading it aloud.

"I love my parents and my brothers and sisters very much. I think of them every day. After I graduated from college I felt proudly and my family was happy for me. But then I received the news; I was assigned to Hunan Medical College. I am from Beijing, far away from here. Beijing is a wonderful place and Hunan is a terrible place. The weather and general situation is terrible.

"I tried to convince the Leaders to change it so I could stay with my family but it was impossible, and I must go where the Party sends me. When I got on the train, I did not know when I could come back again, and I cried for a thousand miles.

"Several years later our college gave me permission to visit my family. When the train arrived in Beijing, my whole family was at the station to meet me. I had so much to tell them, I had planned on the whole train ride all the stories I would tell them, but when I saw them, no words came out from my mouth. I only stood there and tears fell out of my eyes like rain. This was my happiest moment."

Teacher Zhu read last.

"My story is very common, because I am a very common man. In the winter of 1975 I traveled to Beijing. My relative in Beijing invited me to a restaurant famous for its Beijing duck. On a cold day we walked in the restaurant. Inside was warm and comfortable! We sat down and the banquet started. First we ate cold dishes, such as marinated pig stomach and sea slugs. Then we had steamed fish, then at last the duck arrived! The skin was brown and crisp and shiny. In my mouth it was like clouds disappearing. The sauces were various and delicious, and each piece of skin we put in a *bing*—Teacher Mark, how do you say *bing* in English?

"We call them pancakes."

"Pancakes. Each piece of skin we put in a 'pancakes' with sauce and scallions. Afterwards we had the duck meat with vegetables. After that we had duck bone soup and fruits."

He seemed to be finished, but then he put his composition down and smiled **sheepishly** at me.

"Teacher Mark. I have to tell you something. **Actually** this story is true, but actually I have never been to Beijing. Can you guess? My wife went to Beijing and had this duck. But she often tells me about it again and again, and I think, even though I was not there, it is my happiest moment."

(723 words)

Freewriting

Write for 15 minutes about anything that comes into your mind related to this reading. You may wish to write about something that happened to you or to someone you know.

After you finish, read your writing to some of your classmates, and listen to their writings. Talk about the interesting points in each of the writings, and ask questions if you don't understand or if you would like to know more about something.

Quotations

Read these quotations, and explain what they mean:

"The roots of education are bitter, but the fruits are sweet."

ARISTOTLE

"Education makes a people easy to lead, but difficult to drive; easy to govern, but impossible to enslave."

Lord BROUGHAM, 1828

"You can lead a horse to water, but you can't make him drink; you can send your son to college, but you can't make him think."

PROVERB

Sports

Before You Begin

DISCUSS THESE QUESTIONS WITH YOUR CLASSMATES:

1. Are sports popular in your country?
2. Which are the most popular sports?
3. Do you like sports?
4. Which ones do you like best?
5. Do you play any sports? Which ones?
6. What are some of the reasons that people enjoy sports?

C H A P T E R O N E

Sports Around the World

A nne Haddad and Joseph Lee are now talking about sports. **Read this dialogue with a partner.**

Joseph:　Do you like to play volleyball, Anne?

Anne:　　Yeah, I used to play sometimes in high school.

Joseph:　Well, would you like to play tomorrow afternoon? We need another person on my team.

Anne:　　Well, I don't know. I like to play, but I'm not a very good player. How good is the team?

Joseph:　Not that good. We're certainly not professionals! We just play for fun on Sunday afternoons.

Anne:　　Well, it sounds like fun—as long as it's not too **competitive.**

Joseph:　Oh, we're **definitely** not too competitive. We just play for fun.

Anne:　　Okay. It sounds good!

Joseph:　Of course, we do like to win. . . .

First Reading: Getting the Main Idea

Read through the following passage. Try to understand the meaning, and don't stop to look up new words. Take as much time as you need to complete your first reading.

The Popularity of Sports

Sports are **extremely** popular in most countries around the world. People feel **excited** and happy when their favorite team wins, and they feel **sad** and **disappointed** when their favorite team loses. Sports make everyday life more fun and more interesting. In addition, playing sports can be a good way of getting exercise, **relaxing**, and helping us stay **healthy** and **in shape**.

We don't know exactly how and when sports first started. However, in both the East and the West, the history of sports is very long and has always been an extremely important part of every culture. In the beginning, sports were much more than just **entertainment**. They were connected to religion, and people **participated** in games as a way to try to **influence** nature. For example, the Zunis, a Mexican tribe that lived in a very dry area, took part in games because they believed that the gods would send them rain if they played well and won. Then their corn crops would grow, and they would be able to **survive**. In southern Nigeria, young men took part in wrestling matches, and they also believed that their games could **magically influence** the growth of their crops. Because the **outcome** of the games was so important to their future, very large crowds of people gathered to watch and to give support and **encouragement** to the participants. For both the participants and the **spectators**, games were a matter of life and death and a way of trying to influence and control an **uncertain** future. People believed that sports were a gift from the gods and a **form of** religious worship.

The Olympics

Early societies also used sports as training exercises to prepare young men for war and survival. However, as people started to live together more peacefully, sports **festivals**, such as the Olympic Games, were developed as a **peaceful substitute** for war. In other words, these competitions brought different groups of people together peacefully and took the place of war in the society.

Everybody today knows about the Olympics, especially in this age of television. Every four years, we have the opportunity to watch the best sportsmen and sportswomen in the world **compete** against each other in these international games. Probably you have watched **athletes** from your country taking part in these competitions. If so, you know the excitement and **pride** you can feel when a person or a team from your country participates in the Olympics and does well.

The Olympic Games first began in 776 B.C. in Greece, originally as a religious **celebration** in **honor** of the god Zeus. It was the highest honor to be allowed to participate in the Olympics, and only males of good **character** were chosen to take

part in these games. Women, **slaves**, non-Greeks, and people who had ever been in any kind of trouble in society could not participate. As a matter of fact, women were not even allowed to watch the Olympic Games after a certain point because the participants **performed in the nude.**

At the first Olympic Games, in 776 B.C., there was only one event, a footrace of 200 meters. After the thirteenth Olympic Games, however, other events were included: wrestling, discus throwing, and chariot racing. The competitions were held every four years, just as they are today.

The Olympic athletes had a ten-month training period to prepare for the competition. They **devoted** themselves entirely to their training during this time. They ate and drank a special diet (cheese, wine, and some meat) and followed a difficult but carefully designed training program. They prayed that the gods would allow them to win, but only if they were good enough and **deserved** to win. The athletes did not work. Instead, their families and their home city-states **supported** them completely.

Olympic **winners** were given many **gifts** and special **privileges** by their city-states. They did not have to pay **taxes,** and they were given the best seats in the local theater for the rest of their lives. Poets wrote poems **praising** them for their victory. The whole society honored them and looked up to them as heroes and as **role models.** People believed that the winners were not only chosen by the gods, but that they became like gods themselves through winning.

Over a period of time, Greece lost power, and Rome gained power. As a result of this **shift** in power, the games gradually changed from religious festivals to **carnivals** and **circuses** to **amuse** people and to keep their minds off problems in society. Finally, Emperor Theodosius II of Rome stopped the Olympics in 394 A.D. He was a Christian, and he believed that the Olympic Games were bad for a Christian society because they encouraged people to think about the body rather than the **spirit.** By that time, the Olympics had lasted for more than 1,000 years. That was the end of the Olympic Games for the next fifteen centuries.

The Modern Olympics

In 1896, the modern Olympics began. Baron Pierre de Coubertin of France was the father of the modern Olympics. He believed that international games would be a good way to create peace and good feelings among people from different countries. Because the early Olympics had begun in Greece, King George I of Greece was invited to open the first modern Olympic Games in 1896. More than 50,000 people attended.

The modern Olympic Games were different from the early Olympics in a number of important ways. First of all, there was no longer any connection with religion. Second, the Games were not **limited** to Greeks. They were international, and one of their main goals was to **promote** world **peace** and understanding among people from different countries. England, France, Germany, Denmark, Hungary, Switzerland, and the United States sent teams to the 1896 Olympics. After that, athletes continued to compete in games every four years except for three times during times of war: The First World War **prevented** the Olympic meeting of 1916, and the Second World War stopped the 1940 and 1944 meetings. Sometimes individual countries have chosen not to send their athletes to the Olympics. In this way, they make a political statement of some sort to the world.

Women in the Olympics

In ancient Greece, women were not allowed to take part in the Olympic Games or even to watch them as spectators. However, they held their own games, which were called "Heraea," and they were in honor of the goddess Hera, the queen of heaven. These games also took place every four years up until the time of the Roman conquest of Greece.

Women were first invited to participate in the modern Olympics in 1912. Since then, women's events have become very important and popular. People look forward to watching women's gymnastics and volleyball events in particular because women have shown great sports ability in these events, but women excel in many other sports as well. Girls and boys all around the world today can admire and look up to women athletes in the Olympics, and this changes their ideas about what women can do with their lives.

(1,203 words)

Second Reading: Filling in the Gaps

Read the passage a second time to help you understand it better. After you finish the second reading, work with another student in your class and try to guess the meanings of new words.

Third Reading: Putting the Information Together

Read the passage a third time as quickly as you can. Try to understand the meaning of the new words in their context as you read. Reading the passage a third time will help you understand the ideas and learn new vocabulary at the same time.

1. Understanding Ideas and Vocabulary

Choose or supply the correct answers. Talk about your answers with your classmates.

1. What does 776 B.C. mean?

    a.   776 years before the birth of Jesus Christ.
    b.   776 years after the birth of Christ.
    c.   the same thing as 776.

2. The modern Olympics are different from the early Olympics in a number of ways. What are some of the differences?

    _____

    _____

    _____

3. Draw a line from each item on the left to the words on the right that mean almost the same thing.

1.	394 A.D.	a.	when women first appeared in the Olympics
2.	1912	b.	the end of the early Olympics
3.	1896	c.	when the Olympics first began in ancient Greece
4.	776 B.C.	d.	times when Olympic games were canceled due to war
5.	1916, 1940, 1944	e.	the beginning of the modern Olympics

4. Some of these statements are true, and some of them are not true. Read each statement carefully. Write **true** or **false** in each blank.

_____ a. Women did not participate in sports until 1896.

_____ b. Religion is an important part of the modern Olympics.

_____ c. The early Olympics were international. In other words, athletes from many nations participated in them.

_____ d. The early Olympics gradually lost their religious purpose under Roman rule.

_____ e. The modern Olympics are the same as the early Olympics.

5. Cross out the word or phrase that is **not** like the other two words or phrases. You may look up words in the glossary or in your dictionary.

a. to participate—to watch—to take part

b. winning—losing—victory

c. spectator—participant—contestant

d. Heraea—the Olympics—athletes

e. competition—occasion—contest

2. Let's Talk!

These questions ask you about sports in your country. Talk about these questions with two or three of your classmates. After you finish talking, write your answers on the blank lines.

1. What is your favorite sport?

   _____

   Have you ever played this sport? If so, explain when and where.

   _____

2. What are the most popular sports in your country?

   _____

   Are these individual or team sports? _____

   What is your favorite team? _____

3. Vocabulary and Structure Practice

Choose the correct word and write it on the line. Talk about your answers with your group.

Sports are popular all around _____ (1) world. Some people
$\overline{a—an—the}$

like to _____ (2) their favorite teams on television.
$\overline{watch—look—find}$

Others _____ (3) to take part in sports themselves. We know
$\overline{likes—like—liked}$

that people _____ (4) enjoyed watching and taking part in
$\overline{has—have—had}$

sports for thousands _____ (5) years. For example, the Olympic
$\overline{in—for—of}$

Games first _____ (6) in Greece in 776 _____ (7)
$\overline{begin—began—begun}$ $\overline{A.D.—B.C.}$

and after that, Olympic athletes competed every _____ (8)
$\overline{two—four—six}$

years for more than a _____ (9) years. The early
$\overline{hundred—thousand—million}$

Olympic Games were religious _____ (10) in
$\overline{festivals—circuses—carnivals}$

honor of the god Zeus. The _____ (11) trained for ten
$\overline{athlete—athletes}$

months _____ (12) the Games. Their families
after—during—before

supported them so they _____ (13) have to work. The
did—did not—liked

_____ (14) were heroes _____ (15) the
supporters—heroes—athletes *in—from—by*

society, and everybody admired and looked _____ (16) to them
down—up—over

and gave them gifts _____ (17) special privileges. In order to
with—or—and

participate _____ (18) the Games, you had to be
with—for—in

_____ (19) male. _____ (20) could not participate
a—an—the *Men—Women—Greeks*

even as spectators. However, they had their own games,

called "Heraea."

Professional Sports

R ead this sports survey and answer each question by drawing a circle around "yes" or "no." Talk about your answers with two or three of your classmates.

1. Sports of all kinds are very important in a society.   yes   no

2. I like professional sports better than amateur sports.   yes   no

3. Most young people admire and look up to professional players as heroes and role models.   yes   no

4. Professional players have the responsibility to be good role models for young people.   yes   no

5. Professional sports are more like big businesses than true sports.   yes   no

First Reading: Getting the Main Idea

Read through the following passage. Try to understand the meaning, and don't stop to look up new words. Take as much time as you need to complete your first reading.

Amateur and Professional Sports

There are two kinds of sports, "amateur" and "professional." The main difference between them is that **amateurs** do not receive money for competing in sports and professionals do. For example, Olympic athletes are amateurs, so they usually cannot receive money for their participation. The word *amateur* comes from the Latin *amare,* meaning "to love"; in other words, amateurs are supposed to play because they love the game.

On the other hand, professional athletes are paid to compete, and some of the top professionals earn millions of dollars a year.

Professional sports give great athletes the opportunity to play sports as a career and to earn and save money for the future. As long as they can continue to play the game well, they can continue to perform. We as spectators have the opportunity to watch wonderful performances by our favorite professional athletes for the price of an admission ticket or by turning on the television.

However, there are some problems with professional sports. Sports are supposed to encourage the development of good character and **"sportsmanship."** Some professional athletes **demonstrate admirable skill** in playing their game, but their life off the field or the court is not very admirable and, in some cases, **shocking** and even **criminal.** Some have been charged with criminal acts, such as rape, assault and battery, and using illegal drugs. Even when playing the game, they may **swear** at the other players and officials and use **obscene gestures** and language that do not demonstrate sportsmanship.

What is the role of professional athletes in modern society? Should they be role models for young people to admire, look up to and **imitate**, as the early Olympic athletes were? Or do they just have to be top athletes and play their sport well? There is a lot of controversy around these questions. Arthur Ashe, the great American tennis player who died in 1993, **criticized** the behavior of some of his fellow athletes. He said that many of them did not take their responsibilities as sports stars seriously, and, consequently, they were poor models for young people to follow.

Professional athletes do not agree on what their role should be. Charles Barkley, a star basketball player, believes that his role is to be a great basketball player, not a role model for young people. As he said, "I'm not paid to be a role model. I'm paid to **wreak havoc** on the basketball court."[1] Barkley believes that what he does in his **private life** is his own business and should not be important to anyone else. On the other hand, Karl Malone, another star basketball player, disagrees with Barkley. He says that sports stars are role models for people even if they don't want to be. As Malone commented to Barkley, "Charles, you can **deny** being a role model all you want, but I don't think it's your

---

[1] **I'm paid to wreak havoc on the basketball court**—I am paid to destroy the opposition (the other team) in a basketball game.

[2] From "I'm Not a Role Model," *Newsweek,* June 28, 1993, pp. 56–57.

Roger Clemens earns millions of dollars each year as a pitcher for the Boston Red Sox.

decision to make. We don't *choose* to be role models, we are *chosen*. Our only choice is whether to be a good role model or a bad one."[2]

What do children and teenagers think about the role of professional athletes in society? They have different opinions about this matter, just as adults do. Some of them believe that sports stars should try to be role models in all aspects of their life because kids look up to them and want to be like them. However, others believe that sports stars are just people, except for their outstanding skill in their sport. They believe that stars should not be expected to be perfect and that whatever they do in their private life is not important and is just their own business. They think **kids** will try to imitate their performance in their sport, not their behavior in their private life. In other words, kids will try to play basketball like Michael Jordan, but they won't become gamblers because Michael Jordan is a gambler.

Violence in Professional Sports

Another dark side of professional sports is the **atmosphere** of **violence** that surrounds them. There have been many unfortunate cases of spectators getting into fights and hurting and even killing each other at professional sports events. In soccer, for example, a terrible **tragedy** occurred at Heysel Stadium in Brussels before the European Cup Finals in 1985. An English soccer team was playing an Italian soccer team for the European championship. The English fans started a fight with the Italian fans. As the fans **pushed** and **shoved** each other against the stadium walls, one of the walls **collapsed.** As a result, more than 50 people were killed, and many others were badly injured. Why did this happen? What caused this terrible violence? We still do not completely know the answers to these questions, but it is unfortunately not unusual for fights to **occur** at sports **events.**

Professional sports have become more like businesses than pleasure sports. Everything is money, money, money. Teams have to win a lot of games to keep their fans happy, or the fans won't come to their games. Then the team can't earn enough money to pay its expenses. This puts a lot of pressure on the players. They feel they have to win all the time, and winning becomes more

important than anything else. In sports, there is an old **saying:** "It is not important if you win or lose; what is important is the way you play the game." In professional sports, this saying is no longer true, unfortunately. Winning is the most important thing in professional sports.

(957 words)

Second Reading: Filling in the Gaps

Read the passage a second time to help you understand it better. After you finish the second reading, work with another student in your class and try to guess the meanings of new words.

Third Reading: Putting the Information Together

Read the passage a third time as quickly as you can. Try to understand the meaning of the new words in their context as you read. Reading the passage a third time will help you understand the ideas and learn new vocabulary at the same time.

1. Understanding Ideas and Vocabulary

Choose or supply the correct answers to the questions. Talk about your answers with your classmates.

1. What is the main difference between amateur sports and professional sports?

    _____

    _____

2. What are some of the good things about professional sports?

    _____

    _____

3. What are some of the bad things about professional sports?

    _____

    _____

4. Some of these statements are true, and some of them are not true. Read each statement carefully. Write **true** or **false** in each blank.

    _____ a. Amateur athletes receive money for taking part in sports.

    _____ b. Professional athletes receive money for taking part in sports.

    _____ c. Sports, especially professional sports, sometimes create an atmosphere of violence.

    _____ d. On professional teams, winning is often more important than sportsmanship.

    _____ e. The passage says we should not have professional sports.

5. Cross out the word that is **not** like the other two words. You may look up words in the glossary or in your dictionary.

    a. peace—violence—fighting
    b. worry—pressure—pleasure
    c. career—profession—amateur
    d. contestant—fan—supporter
    e. sportsmanship—sports—good character

2. Let's Talk!

These questions ask you about sports, especially professional sports. Talk about your answers with two or three of your classmates. After you finish talking, write your answers on the blank lines.

1. Are you a sports fan? _____ What is your favorite sport, and what is your favorite team?

    _____

    _____

    _____

    Why do you like this team?

    _____

    _____

Win or lose, do you still like your team? Explain.

_____

_____

_____

2. Some athletes have had drug, alcohol, and other types of problems. Can you think of an athlete who has had some sort of problem? _____ Who is the athlete, and what was the problem?

_____

_____

_____

3. Do you think people should expect professional athletes to be role models for young people? _____ Charles Barkley said that he is paid just to be a great basketball player and that he is not paid to be a role model. Do you agree or disagree with Barkley? Explain.

_____

_____

_____

4. Have you ever seen or heard about violence among fans at a sports event? _____ Explain.

_____

_____

5. "Professional sports are business, not sports." Do you agree or disagree with this statement? Explain. _____

_____

_____

_____

3. Vocabulary and Structure Practice

Choose the correct word and write it on the line. Talk about your answers with your group.

Sports _____ (1) very important in most societies.
is—are—were

People enjoy taking _____ (2) in sports and watching
place—part—time

_____ (3) as spectators. Both amateur _____ (4)
it—them—these   *and—but—or*

professional sports have an important place in society. In recent years,

however, there _____ (5) been some disturbing problems in
have—has—had

_____ (6) sports. There have been many
amateur—professional—all

_____ (7) in newspapers and magazines about professional
article—articles

_____ (8) being involved in gambling, drugs, and other
player—players

_____ (9) activities. _____ (10) players are not
criminal—criminals   *This—That—These*

good role models for young people, many people _____ (11).
think—thought

_____ (12) problem in _____ (13) sports is
Another—Other   *professional—professionals*

the atmosphere of violence at many of the games. Fans sometimes get

into _____ (14) and get injured or even _____ (15)
fight—fights   *kill—killing—killed*

in some cases.

CHAPTER THREE

The History of Football

Look carefully at this picture before you begin reading.

In this painting, members of the Sioux tribe are shown playing lacrosse, a game that was invented by Native Americans.

First Reading: Getting the Main Idea

Read through the following passage. Try to understand the meaning, and don't stop to look up new words. Take as much time as you need to complete your first reading.

Football: What It Is and How It Started

Football is an **ancient** game, and most cultures around the world have had some form of this game. Long ago in **primitive** cultures, the ball in the game represented the sun, and people believed that the success of their crops depended on the way the players threw or kicked the ball during the game. In some cases, the **goal** was a tree, which was a **symbol** of growing things. If a player hit the tree with the ball, it meant that the crops would grow.

Football was played in China as early as the second century, and it was **similar** in some ways to soccer[3] as it is played today. In the Chinese football game, the players used their feet and bodies to move the ball, but never their hands. The goal was a hole in a net made from silk, and the teams competed with each other to try to kick the ball through this hole. The winners received a silver cup filled with fruit or wine. The losers received a "prize" too: They were beaten up by the winning team!

What were the balls made of? In the British Museum in London, there is an **exhibit** of a number of ancient balls from various cultures around the world. Thousands of years ago, the Egyptians made balls out of soft leather or fine linen, and they filled them with cut **reed** or **straw** to make them round and hard. In other cultures, the balls were filled with earth, grain, bits and pieces of plants, and sometimes even pieces of metal. The Mayas made their balls out of solid rubber.

Some historians believe that the first balls were actually heads! A group of people would cut off the head of one of their enemies and then use this head as a football, supposedly to **celebrate** their **victory** over their **enemy** and to bring them **luck** and **prosperity.** In an ancient story from Great Britain, for example, the storyteller explains how the Britons **cut off** the head of a Danish invader and later played football with it. There is some **evidence** that animal heads were also sometimes used as footballs.

Ball games were connected to **fertility** in primitive societies. People believed that success in ball games would help their crops to grow and help the players to produce children as well. From earliest days, tribes divided their players into teams: unmarried men against married men or unmarried women against married women. It was believed that throwing the ball (the symbol of life and fertility) **back and forth** among these groups would help the players to become stronger and to produce healthy children in the future.

Football was popular in both ancient Greece and Rome. In the Greek version of football, the players on one team tried to

---

[3] **Soccer**—this sport is known as *football* outside the United States.

carry a ball across a line in the **opposing** team's **territory**, and the opposing team tried to keep them from crossing the line. This **version** of football is similar in some ways to today's American football. The Roman football game was like the Greek game. The players had to throw the ball from one to another to try to get the ball over the other team's **baseline**. In this game, players were not allowed to kick the ball. Galen, a famous doctor in the second century in Rome, wrote about how football helped the players become stronger and healthier. Many other writers wrote about how football helped prepare young men for war and taught them the skills they needed for survival.

In England in the Middle Ages, whole towns played football on certain holidays, such as **Shrove Tuesday**, sometimes with as many as 500 players at one time. The goals were placed at the opposite ends of the town, and sometimes the game lasted all day. Everything was allowed: You could kick, trip, hit, or bite your opponent. In fact, you could do anything you wanted in order to get or keep the ball. Consequently, players were often seriously injured and sometimes even killed in these **rough** games. Also, there was a lot of property damage, and windows were often broken throughout the town. Finally, in 1314, these games had become so violent and dangerous that King Edward II made a law saying that people could not play football in the future and that anyone who broke this law would be sent to prison:

> Forasmuch as there is great noise in the city, caused by hustling over large balls from which many evils might arise which God forbid, we commend and forbid, on behalf of the King, on pain of imprisonment, such game to be used in the city in the future.[4]

This law kept people from playing football for a while, but it was not successful for long because everyone, even priests and monks, had a strong attraction to the game. Finally, in 1603, when King James I came into power, football was allowed again, and people were even encouraged to play it. As time went on, rules were added to the game to make it **safer** and more **orderly**, and players were limited in what they could and could not do to get and keep the ball.

Football originally meant "a game played with a ball on foot" **—as opposed to** a game played on horseback, such as polo.

---

[4] "Because playing football causes so much noise in the city as well as many other bad things that God says people should not do, people are not allowed to play football in the city in the future. If they do, they will be sent to prison."

In this picture, ancient Mayans are shown playing a game similar to modern basketball.

Soccer, as played throughout the world today, is closest to the original football. Rugby, American football, and Australian Rules football all come from soccer and are later versions of the game. (903 words)

Second Reading: Filling in the Gaps

Read the passage a second time to help you understand it better. After you finish the second reading, work with another student in your class and try to guess the meanings of new words.

Third Reading: Putting the Information Together

Read the passage a third time as quickly as you can. Try to understand the meaning of the new words in their context as you read. Reading the passage a third time will help you understand the ideas and learn new vocabulary at the same time.

1. Understanding Ideas and Vocabulary

Choose or supply the correct answers. Talk about your answers with your classmates.

1. In this passage, *football* means

    a. any game played with a ball.
    b. any game where a ball is kicked.
    c. any game played on foot with a ball.

2. What did King James I do in 1603?

    a. He made a law against football to prevent violence and property damage.
    b. He allowed football again but discouraged people from playing it.
    c. He not only allowed football again but also encouraged people to play it.

3. What did it mean when a player hit the tree (the goal) with the ball? Did it mean something good or something bad? Explain.

    _____

    _____

    _____

4. Some of these statements are true, and some of them are not true. Read each statement carefully. Write **true** or **false** in each blank.

    _____ a. In football, as played in China in the second century, players were not allowed to kick the ball.
    _____ b. Egyptians made balls out of solid rubber thousands of years ago.
    _____ c. The ball used in games was originally a fertility symbol representing the sun and life.
    _____ d. In 1314, a law was passed in England making it illegal (against the law) for people to play football.
    _____ e. In the Middle Ages in England, players were not allowed to kick or hit players on the other team.

5. Cross out the word or phrase that is **not** like the other two words or phrases. You may look up words in the glossary or in your dictionary.

    a.   legal—illegal—not legal

    b.   opposing team—losing team—the other team

    c.   prosperity—wealth—health

    d.   consequently—as a result—on the other hand

    e.   to kill—to injure—to hurt

2. Let's Talk!

These questions ask you more about sports. Talk about your answers with two or three of your classmates. After you finish talking, write your answers on the blank lines.

1. What was the most interesting part of this reading for you? Why? What did you learn from this reading?

    _____

    _____

    _____

2. Why did King Edward II make a law in 1314 against playing football? What was he trying to prevent?

    _____

    _____

    _____

3. Football originally was "a game played on foot with a ball." Make a list of as many games played on foot with a ball as you can think of. Compare your list with the lists of your classmates.

    _____

    _____

    _____

4. "The important thing about sports is not winning or losing. The important thing is how you play the game." Do you agree or disagree? Why? Explain.

_____

_____

_____

3. Vocabulary Practice: Word Forms

Read each sentence carefully. Then choose the correct word form from the list, and write it on the line. *(Note:* This list has only the most common forms. It is not a complete list of all forms.) Talk about your answers with your group.

Word Form List

	Noun	Verb	Adjective	Adverb
1.	belief	to believe	believable	—
2.	success	to succeed	successful	successfully
3.	winner	to win	winning	—
4.	division	to divide	—	—
5.	history historian	—	historical	—

1. Mr. Assad has a strong _____ in his religion.

   I don't _____ I know your name.

   Do you think his story is _____?

2. You must work hard if you want to _____.

   Jenny Cheung is a _____ scientist.

   They completed their schoolwork _____.

   Everybody is interested in _____.

3. The _____ soccer team came from Brazil.

    We played tennis very well, but we didn't _____.

    Who was the _____ in the World Cup last year?

4. In elementary school, children learn addition, subtraction

    multiplication, and _____.

    If you _____ the number 120 by 2, the answer is
    60.

5. I am interested in the _____ of ancient Egypt.

    A specialist in the field of history is called a _____.

    Kristin likes to visit _____ places when she travels.

E X P A N S I O N   A C T I V I T I E S

Interview: Sports

You have discussed your views on sports in the "Let's Talk!" exercises above. Now interview a classmate about an athlete in his or her culture. If possible, try to choose someone who comes from a different background than you do.

Planning and Conducting the Interview

A. Plan your interview. Before you interview the person, think about the questions you want to ask. Write out these questions on a piece of paper. You may want to begin with the questions that follow. Then work with a partner to get ideas for more questions. Be sure to leave space on your paper for the answers.

1. May I ask you some questions about your favorite athlete?

2. Who is this person and what sport does she or he play?

    _____

    Does this athlete play on a team? If so, which one? _____

3. Why do you admire this person? _____

    _____

4. (Suggestion: You could ask if this person is famous and, if so, why. You could ask about this person's achievements—what they were and when and where they took place. In other words, did this person set any records?)

    _____

    _____

5. (Suggestion: You might want to ask if this person is a good role model for young people and then ask why or why not. You also could ask if it is important for a sportsperson to be a good role model in addition to being a good athlete.)

_____

_____

_____

6. (Suggestion: Ask if there are other interesting and important things about this person.)

_____

_____

_____

Be sure to add other questions you would like to ask in your interview.

B. Choose a classmate to interview.

C. Begin your interview.   Do not try to write complete answers to your questions. Just make notes to help you remember the answers.

Interaction

Work with two or three other classmates. Tell the group about your interview. Tell them the name of the person you interviewed, and then tell them your questions and the answers that the person gave. Be sure to use your notes to help you remember what the person said in the interview.

Special Reading

"Goals" was written by Jesse Lee Hardy after his last game as a high school football star. It is part of an unpublished novel called *The Game: A Life in Progress* that Mr. Hardy wrote in 1991. Mr. Hardy is now a college student, and he plans to become a professional writer.

Goals

I am sitting in an empty stadium after my last high school football game that finished a few hours ago. I'm the quarterback on my team. Well, actually, that's not true now. I was the quarterback because, as I said, this was my last game. It was the league championship. That's a good way to end a high school football career, especially if you win, but even if you don't, it's good to leave at a high point.

I've been sitting here by myself **shivering** in the cold and thinking back over the game and other games I've played in my life. I'm looking at the goal and thinking how it always seemed to reach out and pull me with a secret, magical **force.** I remember all the times I closed my eyes on the field and thought, "There has to be a way to get the ball across that line. There has to be a way." Even if I didn't find the way, I always believed there was a way. Now, I'm not so sure.

I was 8 when I first started playing football. My dad loved football, and he would practice with me at home—passing, catching, running. We'd practice almost every evening until it got too dark. My mom would try to get us to stop so I could do my homework, but my dad would tell me, "Never mind. You can do that later," and we'd just go on playing. He tried to teach me everything he knew about the game. "Just remember: don't ever **give up.**" "Stay in the game. Don't lose your concentration." "Go out there and give 110 percent every time." Well, that was a long time ago, but I still hear his words ringing in my ears.

My mom told me in junior high, "You're not going to be big enough to play football in high school. You have to think about your schoolwork and try to make something out of yourself. Otherwise, you'll be **stuck** working in a factory all your life." She meant well, I know, and she probably knew what she was talking about because she'd worked as a waitress most of her life. And she was right about the size thing too. I was not very big. But she was wrong about other things. I made the high school team when I was just a sophomore because I was fast and I was smart—not in a school way, but in a football way. I could communicate with a football better than I could with a person.

Then things started to **fall apart.** My mom and my dad **split up.** My dad got married again. I didn't see him much after that, but he'd come to my games and we'd talk a little afterwards. "How's it going, **pal?**" he'd ask. "It's okay, Dad," I'd say. After a while, we couldn't think of anything to say, so he'd talk football to me for a while: "Now, just remember, don't give up. Keep your eyes on the ball and don't lose your **concentration.**" Things like that. I'd **nod** and say, "Yeah, Dad. That's right." And then he'd **clap** me on the shoulder and say, "**So long,** pal."

After a while, he started missing some of my games. Once in a while he wouldn't show up and then he gradually started missing more and more. He always seemed real glad to see me when he came, but he just didn't come that much. My mom and I never talked about this, but I knew what she was thinking, and I didn't like it. I mean, things can happen. Maybe he had to work another **shift.** You can't always control things like that. She wouldn't understand though because she's the type of person who will just **hang in** there. She's kind of hard and tough sometimes, but you can depend on her to be there, even if you don't want her around. I mean, she doesn't even like or understand football, but she'd never miss a game. She could have the flu and a temperature of 102. It wouldn't matter. She'd still be there. It's hard to explain why that **upsets** me so much.

I had a lot on my mind before the game today. I don't like things to end, I guess, and this was the last game, and it was the league championship. I was talking to myself and reminding myself about what to do and not to do. I didn't sleep at all last night, and when the sun came up this morning, I reached the point where I just wanted it all to be over, finished, done. But then when the game started, my mind became empty; it was like sand draining out of an **hour glass.** Everything dropped away from me. I just lived in this game, this moment. I didn't have any other existence. I didn't hear the crowd, I didn't feel the cold or the pain, I never felt tired. I just kept my eyes on the ball, and it was just me and the ball and, inside, a soft, white light showing me the way to the goal. It was a beautiful, empty feeling.

It's all over now, and it's really getting cold up here. It's starting to snow. The sun's almost gone, and I can barely see the **goalposts.** Now it's dark and I'm sitting here all alone. Well, I guess it's time to say good-bye and move on.

(919 words)

Freewiting

Write for 15 minutes about anything that comes into your mind related to this reading passage. You may want to write about something that happened to you or to someone you know.

After you finish, read your writing to some of your classmates, and listen to their writings. Talk about the interesting points in each of the writings, and ask questions if you don't understand or if you would like to know more about something.

Quotations

Read these quotations, and explain what they mean:

> "I always believe in my heart that through sport one day all the people will be together. Through the political way we can never come together. I always felt that if I were on the political side I could never get the same treatment in Russia or Red China or in Japan or South America. But as I was involved in soccer I had the open door—everyplace."
>
> PÉLÉ

> "Football today is far too much a sport for the few who can play it well; the rest of us, and too many of our children, get our exercise from climbing up the steps in stadiums, or from walking across the room to turn on our television sets. And this is true for one sport after another."
>
> JOHN F. KENNEDY

> "The important thing is not winning, but taking part, for the essential thing in life is not so much conquering as fighting well."
>
> THE BISHOP OF PENNSYLVANIA
> (referring to the 1908 Olympics in London)

Superstitions

Before You Begin

DISCUSS THESE QUESTIONS WITH YOUR CLASSMATES:

1. Are you afraid of black cats? Do you believe that they bring bad luck?
2. Do you have a "lucky" number?
3. What do you think about the number 13?
4. What is a superstition? What is a common superstition in your culture?

"Mirror, mirror on the wall, who's the fairest of them all?"

Magic and Mirrors

R ead this paragraph and discuss its meaning with a partner.

"Fairies? No, of course I don't believe in them," said the old woman **indignantly** when questioned by one of the workers from the Irish **Folklore Commission**. "But they're there," she added in a **lowered** voice. That old Irish woman was in the same boat[1] with Charles Anderson Dana, **noted** American **man of letters**, who once said, "No, I don't believe in ghosts but I've been afraid of them all my life."

> —from *The Soup Stone*, by Maria Leach
> (New York: Funk & Wagnalls, 1954)

First Reading: Getting the Main Idea

Read through the following passage. Try to understand the meaning, and don't stop to look up new words. Take as much time as you need to complete your first reading.

What Are Superstitions?

Superstitions have been part of life since the beginning of human history, and even in today's age of science and technology, most of us are secretly superstitious about certain things, even though we may **pretend** not to be. We may have lucky numbers or colors. We may wear a certain shirt or blouse or a special ring to bring us luck on an important occasion. Just to be on the safe side, we may cross our fingers for luck, **avoid** the number 13, or cross the street when we see a black cat.

What are superstitions—and why are people superstitious? The *American Heritage Dictionary* defines superstition in this way:

---

[1] **in the same boat**—in the same position

su·per·sti·tion (sōō´per-stĭsh´ən) *n.* **1.** A belief that some action or circumstance not **logically** related to a course of events influences its **outcome.**
2. Any belief, practice, or **rite** unreasonably **upheld** by faith in magic, chance, or dogma. . . .

Since the beginning of time, people have believed that powers (**gods, ghosts,** spirits, **witches**) could **affect** their lives in both good ways and bad ways and that by doing certain things in a certain way, it might be possible to get on the good side of these **invisible** powers. In other words, if you did what they wanted you to do, no matter how **strange** or **ridiculous** it might be, then they would take care of you, or at least they would leave you alone and not do anything bad to you.

Mirrors

Mirrors have always been regarded as having special powers. The superstition that breaking a mirror is bad luck is very, very old, and it can be found in some form in most cultures around the world. But, as a matter of fact, the first mirrors could not really be broken because they were made of water. People looked at themselves in lakes and **ponds** and rivers because they believed that their **reflection** in the water could tell them about their future. If the water was **calm** and the reflection was clear, this was considered a good sign, meaning that good things would happen to the person. On the other hand, if the water was **rough** and the reflection was **distorted** and hard to see, this was a sign that the future would be bad.

In the sixth century B.C., the Romans were reading water fortunes. You could go to a **seer,** a person with special powers, and have the seer tell you what your future would be. The seer would have you hold a bowl of water and look into it, and then he or she would study your reflection and tell you what was going to happen to you. If you happened to drop the bowl, it meant that you had no future, a very bad sign.

People had the idea from ancient times that a person's reflection or **image** was actually the person's **soul** and that the soul **existed** outside the body in the reflection. Therefore, if the mirror broke (or the water bowl was dropped), it meant that the soul would be destroyed and the person would soon die. In many cultures, people believed that it was dangerous for people to look at their own image too long. This was because they believed the soul in the reflected image could **draw** the life out of the person.

The Basutos, a Bantu tribe in South Africa, believed that crocodiles could **drag** a person's reflection under water and kill it. In many cultures, people believe that if you dream of seeing your reflection in water, it is an **omen** of death.

In the first century B.C., the Romans had changed their ideas about mirror fortunes a little bit. At this time, they believed that a person's health and **fortune** changed every seven years. Therefore, if you broke a mirror, it was not quite so bad as before: You would have seven years of bad health and general bad luck, but at least you probably wouldn't die.

In China, people believed that a well-placed mirror could **protect** you from evil. This was because they thought bad spirits would be **frightened** by their own image in the mirror and would then leave people alone. There is an ancient Chinese saying: "When evil recognizes itself, it destroys itself." Therefore, brass mirrors were often placed in the pointed **gables** of Chinese houses to **scare away** evil **spirits**. Brass mirrors in bedrooms were supposed to protect people while they were sleeping, but they had to be put in just the right place so they would catch the evil spirit's reflection. A mirror set in the wrong place in a bedroom could bring bad luck, so you had to be careful!

Mirrors and Truth

Mirrors are supposed to reveal truth. In the fairy tale "Snow White," the queen looks into her mirror and asks, "Mirror, mirror on the wall, who's the fairest of them all?"[2] Naturally, the queen expects the mirror to answer, "You are the fairest, my dear queen." But the mirror tells the truth—and it tells the queen what she does not want to hear: "You are beautiful, my queen, but Snow White is the fairest of them all."

Mirrors and Omens

A few years before the Spanish Conquest of the Aztec Empire in 1519, a huge bird was brought to the Aztec chief, Montezuma. The bird had a mirror in its head, and when Montezuma looked into the mirror, he saw a great number of armed men.[3] He sent for his wise men to ask them what this omen meant. The bird flew away

---

[2] **Mirror ...who's the fairest of them all?**—Mirror, who is the most beautiful person in the whole country?

[3] *Note:* The "mirror" in the bird's head may have been the bird's eyes instead of a real mirror.

before the wise men could examine what was in the mirror. A few years later, the Spanish **invaded** and **conquered** Montezuma's people. The Aztecs believed that Montezuma's vision had **foretold** their **fate** and that they could not fight against it.

Mirrors and Fire

From earliest days, people in cultures around the world used mirrors to set fires by **focusing** the sun's **rays** on one spot. The Aztecs, the Greeks, the Chinese and many other people used mirrors to perform this magical trick. Because fire has always been so important to life and survival, a person who could start a fire with a mirror had a very high position in ancient societies, at least as high as a top scientist in today's world.
(1,101 words)

Second Reading: Filling in the Gaps

Read the passage a second time to help you understand it better. After you finish the second reading, work with another student in your class and try to guess the meanings of new words.

Third Reading: Putting the Information Together

Read the passage a third time as quickly as you can. Try to understand the meaning of the new words in their context as you read. Reading the passage a third time will help you understand the ideas and learn new vocabulary at the same time.

1. Understanding Ideas and Vocabulary

Choose or supply the correct answers. Talk about your answers with your classmates.

1. In your own words, what does *superstition* mean?

_____

_____

_____

2. According to this passage, most people

   a. are not superstitious today.

   b. are secretly superstitious about some things.

   c. are more superstitious today than they were in the past.

3. Match these words. Draw a line from the word on the left to the words on the right that mean almost the same things.

1.	witch	a.	image in a mirror or in water
2.	vision	b.	not really related or connected; accidental
3.	reflection	c.	a mental image produced by the imagination
4.	frightened	d.	scared; afraid
5.	coincidence	e.	a woman who practices magic

4. Some of these statements are true, and some of them are not true. Read each statement carefully. Write **true** or **false** in each blank.

   _____ a. A ghost is an example of an invisible spirit.

   _____ b. Breaking or cracking a mirror is a good omen.

   _____ c. People have always been superstitious.

   _____ d. In "Snow White," the mirror told a lie (an untruth) to the queen.

   _____ e. When Montezuma saw the armed men in the mirror, it was a bad omen.

5. Cross out the word that is **not** like the other two words. You may look up words in the glossary or in your dictionary.

   a. omen—sign—chance

   b. visible—invisible—not seen

   c. fortune—health—luck

   d. seer—fortune-teller—ghost

   e. clear—unclear—distorted

2. Let's Talk!

These questions ask you about superstitions in your country. Talk about these questions with two or three of your classmates. After you finish talking, write your answers on the blank lines.

1.   What was the most interesting part of this reading for you? Explain why.

_____

_____

2.   What is a common superstition in your culture?

_____

_____

3.   Is it bad luck to crack or break a mirror in your culture? Explain. Are there any other special beliefs about mirrors?

_____

_____

_____

_____

3. Idiomatic Expressions

Idiomatic expressions are special expressions used in language that are often very hard to translate exactly to another language. Read these sentences carefully, and then select from the list a word or phrase that means almost the same thing as the italicized word or phrase. Write the sentence again with the new word or phrase. The first one has been done for you.

to be especially careful   however
not to take any chances   to make a good impression (on)
in the same position (as)

1. I advise you *to play it safe.*

    <u>*I advise you not to take any chances.*</u>

    <u>*I advise you to be especially careful.*</u>

    (*Note:* Both of these sentences are correct.)

2. The old Irish woman was *in the same boat (with)* Charles Anderson Dana.

    _____

    _____

3. I don't really believe in superstitions, but sometimes I act as if I do believe in them *just to be on the safe side.*

    _____

    _____

    _____

    _____

    (*Note:* Write two sentences for this one.)

4. Maya did some extra homework in her math class to try to *get on the good side* of her math teacher.

    _____

    _____

5. If the water was calm and the reflection was clear, this was considered a good sign. *On the other hand,* if the reflection was not clear, this was a sign that the future would be bad.

    _____

    _____

    _____

    _____

C H A P T E R   T W O

The Unlucky Number 13

Joanna Medina is making an airline reservation to return to Spain.
Read this dialogue with a partner.

Clerk: Good afternoon. May I help you?

Joanna: Yes, please. I would like to make a **reservation** to go to Madrid.

Clerk: Do you have a ticket, or do you need to buy one?

Joanna: I have one. I just need to make a reservation.

Clerk: When would you like to **depart?**

Joanna: I'd like to leave at the end of next week.

Clerk: (looking at the computer) I have something **available** next Friday. How is that? Is that all right?

Joanna: Next Friday? Is that the 12th?

Clerk: No, it's the 13th, Friday the 13th.

Joanna: Oh, no! Not that day!

Clerk: (laughing) Why not? Are you superstitious?

Joanna: Not really—but still, I prefer to play it safe! What about Thursday the 12th? Is that possible?

First Reading: Getting the Main Idea

Read through the following passage. Try to understand the meaning, and don't stop to look up new words. Take as much time as you need to complete your first reading.

Unlucky 13

Of all the bad-luck superstitions, studies show that the number 13 is the best known throughout the world. Joanna didn't want to travel on Friday the 13th even though she says she's not superstitious. However, Joanna is not alone. Many people will avoid traveling or **scheduling** an important event on the 13th, especially if it is Friday the 13th—just to be on the safe side!

The 13th Floor—Where Is It?

Skyscrapers are **impressive** symbols of what modern science and technology can do, but it is an interesting fact that superstition continues to exist in the **midst** of these technological **achievements.** If you go into a skyscraper or just a tall building, look to see if it has a 13th floor. The elevator probably goes from 12 to 14—or from 12 to 12-B and then to 14.

The manager of a large, **luxury** apartment building in New York City was asked, "Why is there no 13th floor in this building? Are people still so superstitious in this day and age?" The manager answered, "We had a 13th floor **originally,** and nobody wanted to rent an apartment on that floor. We rented all the apartments on the other floors, and finally we changed the 13th floor to 12B, and we rented every apartment on the floor within one afternoon. So, to answer your question, yes, I think people may be more superstitious than they want to **admit."**

In France, the house number 13 is not used, and in Italy, the number 13 is not used in the national lottery. All around the world, people stay away from this number. They try to avoid traveling on this day or getting married or **undertaking** any other important action.

How this Superstition Began

It is always very hard to find the origin of a particular superstition, but many experts think that the superstition about the number 13 goes back at least several thousand years and, probably, much longer. According to Norse mythology in the pre-Christian era,[4] 12 gods met at Valhalla for a banquet. At the last minute, Loki, the spirit of **evil** and **turmoil,** pushed his way into the banquet uninvited, raising the number of banquet guests from 12 to 13. Loki got into a fight with the other gods, and in the **struggle,** he killed Balder, the favorite of all the gods.

---

[4] **Norse mythology in the pre-Christian era**— folktales in what is now Scandinavia in the period before Christianity began, in other words, more than 2,000 years ago

This superstition spread from Scandinavia through Europe and the Middle East, and it was well-known by the time Christianity began 2,000 years ago. Many people are familiar with the Last Supper, when Christ and his 12 disciples shared a meal together. Only 24 hours after this meal, Christ was **crucified** because he was **betrayed** by Judas, one of his followers, who was at the dinner. From then on, having 13 people to dinner was thought to be a bad omen and an invitation to disaster. Experts in folklore have often compared Judas, the betrayer of Christ, to Loki, the Norse spirit of evil and destruction.

Support for the Superstition

In the year 1798, the editors of a British publication called the *Gentlemen's Magazine* published some statistics to show that in one particular year, one out of every 13 people died. It is interesting to note that they did not publish statistics for other years—where the numbers would have been different. **By the same token**, people will always remember and talk about disasters that happened on Friday the 13th—but they won't remember and talk about the many good things that have occurred on the same day! This is because we all search for evidence to prove what we already believe.

Friday the 13th

Thirteen is unlucky, but Friday the 13th is even more unlucky! Again, this superstition probably goes back to Norse mythology. Friday is named after Frigga, the goddess of love and fertility. When Norse and Germanic tribes became Christian, they gave up their **pagan** gods, including the goddess Frigga. She was called a witch and sent away in shame to the top of a mountain. But people believed that Frigga and 11 other witches—plus the devil, their special guest—got together every Friday to make plans for evil tricks for the following week. For hundreds of years, Friday was called "Witches' Sabbath" in Scandinavia, and people were careful about what they did on this fateful day.

It is interesting to note that children born on Friday, the 13th are considered to be lucky rather than unlucky! It is not clear where this superstition came from, but perhaps people thought it was too **harsh** to call an **innocent** baby unlucky just because of its birthdate.

Superstitions Connected with Other Numbers

Thirteen is not the only number to have superstitions connected with it. Shakespeare once said that there is luck associated with odd numbers (with the exception of 13, of course). The number three is considered by many people to be lucky, and there are many proverbs that mention this number:

The third time's lucky.

If at first you don't succeed, try, try, try again.

In the sixth century B.C., the Greek philosopher Pythagoras said that three was "the perfect number" because it was the sign of completeness and fertility. In some languages, the number *three* and the word *tree* have the same root, and both are ancient signs related to fertility and reproduction. It is said that in most folk medicines, three **ingredients** must be mixed together to produce a cure.

In folktales, the numbers three and seven often appear, and they are usually associated with good luck: "Goldilocks and the Three Bears," "Snow White and the Seven Dwarfs," "The Three Little Pigs." In other forms of literature and in movies, we also find these numbers again and again. In Shakespeare's *King Lear*,

the king has three daughters: Goneril and Regan (the two older, evil daughters) and Cordelia, the youngest, who is the good daughter. In two other well-known plays and movies, *The Seven Samurai* and *Seven Brides for Seven Brothers,* we find the magical number seven. Finally, a seventh child is supposed to have special luck and **healing** powers—and the seventh child of a seventh child is supposed to be an especially gifted person: a magician or a **shaman.**

The number three is important in Christianity in the holy **trinity:** the Father, the Son, and the Holy Ghost. Sigmund Freud, the father of psychoanalysis, said that the human mind is composed of three parts: the id, the ego, and the superego. Classical mythology uses the number three in various symbols; for example, Jupiter holds a bolt of lightning that has three forks. (1,137 words)

Second Reading: Filling in the Gaps

Read the passage a second time to help you understand it better. After you finish the second reading, work with another student in your class and try to guess the meanings of new words.

Third Reading: Putting the Information Together

Read the passage a third time as quickly as you can. Try to understand the meaning of the new words in their context as you read. Reading the passage a third time will help you understand the ideas and learn new vocabulary at the same time.

1. Understanding Ideas and Vocabulary

Choose or supply the correct answers. Talk about your answers with your classmates.

1. The main reason owners of a tall building might not have a thirteenth floor in their building is because

   a. they are superstitious and believe 13 is an unlucky number.

   b. the government does not allow them to use the number 13 in a building.

   c. it's bad for business because many people do not want to have an office or apartment on the 13th floor.

2. Choose the list that contains only odd numbers.

   a.   1, 3, 5, 7, 9, 11, 13, 14, 15, 17, 19

   b.   5, 10, 15, 20, 25, 30, 35, 40, 45

   c.   11, 13, 19, 35, 7, 3, 99, 57, 15, 3

3. Draw a line from each item on the left to the words on the right that mean almost the same thing.

1.	Frigga	a.	Friday
2.	Witches' Sabbath	b.	sometimes called "the perfect number"
3.	13	c.	even more unlucky than 13
4.	3	d.	Nordic goddess of fertility
5.	Friday the 13th	e.	the most unlucky number

4. Some of these statements are true, and some of them are not true. Write **true** or **false** in each blank.

   _____ a.   The words *three* and *tree* are connected in some languages.

   _____ b.   Friday the 13th is considered unlucky.

   _____ c.   Children born on Friday the 13th are supposed to be unlucky.

   _____ d.   Loki is the Nordic god of fertility and good luck.

   _____ e.   Even numbers are supposed to be luckier than odd numbers.

5. Cross out the word that is **not** like the other two words. You may look up words in the glossary or in your dictionary.

   a.   3—7—13

   b.   pleasant—harsh—severe

   c.   fate—destiny—fatal

   d.   growth—disaster—destruction

   e.   unusual ability—gifted—capable

2. Let's Talk!

These questions ask you about number superstitions in your country. Talk about these questions with two or three of your classmates. After you finish talking, write your answers on the blank lines.

1. Does the number 13 have any special meaning in your culture? Explain.

   _____

   _____

   _____

2. Does Friday the 13th have any special meaning in your culture? Explain.

   _____

   _____

   _____

3. Do other numbers (for example, 3, 7, 11) have any special significance in your culture? Explain.

   _____

   _____

   _____

4. Are you superstitious about numbers? Do you have a "lucky" number? Explain and give examples.

   _____

   _____

   _____

   _____

3. Vocabulary and Structure Practice

Choose the correct word and write it on the line. Talk about your answers with your group.

Folktales _____ (1) popular in every culture. People tell
is—are

_____ (2) tales to their children over and over to teach
this—that—these

them _____ (3) cultural lessons. In the Japanese
important—importants

version of "The Three Little Pigs," the lesson _____ (4) that you
is—are—was

must _____ (5) with others and work together
cooperate—cooperating

as _____ (6) team in order to succeed. The three little
a—an—the

_____ (7) are able to _____ (8) the wolf by working
pig—pigs   *destroy—destroyed*

together. In the _____ (9) version of _____ (10)
American—Americans   *a—an—the*

same story, the lesson is that you must be smart and

_____ (11) and able to figure out
independent—independents

_____ (12) and solve them by
problem—problems

_____ (13). This is just one _____ (14) of
yourself—itself—themselves   *example—examples*

how folktales teach the values of each culture.

C H A P T E R ◆ T H R E E

Black Cats

Look carefully at this picture before you begin reading.

First Reading: Getting the Main Idea

Read through the following passage. Try to understand the meaning, and don't stop to look up new words. Take as much time as you need to complete your first reading.

Cat Superstitions

Many people are afraid of cats. They will even cross a street to try to **avoid** meeting a cat, particularly a black cat. On the other hand, other people have great love and affection for cats, and they think that they are **precious** creatures. Cats have been important throughout history, but not always in the same way, and so we will look at two important cat traditions.

Cats in Ancient Egypt

Egyptians began keeping cats as house **pets** about six thousand years ago. They loved cats, and they considered them as the highest form of good luck because cats were supposed to be the favorite companion of the gods. The goddess Basta appeared with the head of a beautiful cat. In ancient Egypt, there were laws to protect cats from death and injury, and Egyptians could be **put to death** for **harming** a cat. When a pet cat died, the whole family **mourned** its death, and they **shaved off** their eyebrows as a sign of mourning and **grief.** They had the cat **embalmed** and wrapped in the finest linen. It was then placed in a **tomb** with its favorite toys and dishes of food. In the late nineteenth century, archaeologists found cat **cemeteries** in Egypt that had been constructed thousands of years before, and they were able to see how important cats had been in ancient Egyptian society by studying these burial **sites.**

Popularity of Black Cats in Other Cultures

Cats were very popular in other cultures as well. In 500 B.C., in ancient China, Confucius had a favorite cat, and he **mentioned** this cat with respect and affection in his writings. In India, cats appear in many Sanskrit writings from more than 2,000 years ago. Much later, in 600 B.C., Mohammed, the prophet who founded the Islamic religion, often **preached** while holding his favorite cat in his arms. At about the same time, the Japanese started keeping cats in places where they kept their most **precious** holy writings because they believed the cats would protect these **manuscripts.** In ancient times, it was considered extremely good luck if a cat crossed your path.

The Chinese have a folktale about cats being the first rulers of the earth. According to the tale, they were able to speak and do everything necessary to govern the entire earth. But, after some time, the cats became tired of this responsibility. They preferred instead to lie in the sun and nap, so they looked around for other animals to take their place. They finally chose humans, and they gave their gift of speech to them. From that time on, according to the tale, cats have looked on calmly and quietly and smiled as humans have tried to run the world.

The French writer, Montaigne, once said, "Who knows whether the cat is not **amusing** herself with me more than I am with her?"

Fear of Cats in the Middle Ages

People started to hate and fear cats in the Middle Ages in Europe, and especially in England. Cats have always been associated with women, and when fear and **hysteria** about witches grew in the Middle Ages, people also started hating and fearing cats, especially black cats. Many people believed that they were witches in **disguise**. All over Europe, cats were burned alive on special days in big public **bonfires** until Louis XIII of France stopped this practice in 1630. To this day, however, many people are afraid of black cats, and they think it is bad luck if a black cat crosses in front of them.

(600 words)

Second Reading: Filling in the Gaps

Read the passage a second time to help you understand it better. After you finish the second reading, work with another student in your class and try to guess the meanings of new words.

Third Reading: Putting the Information Together

Read the passage a third time as quickly as you can. Try to understand the meaning of the new words in their context as you read. Reading the passage a third time will help you understand the ideas and learn new vocabulary at the same time.

1. Understanding Ideas and Vocabulary

Choose or supply the correct answers. Talk about your answers with your classmates.

1. How did the ancient Egyptians feel about cats?

_____

_____

_____

2.   What happened to a person who harmed a cat in ancient Egypt?

_____

_____

3.   In your own words, describe some of the things Egyptians did when a pet cat died.

_____

_____

4.   Why did people hate and fear cats, especially black ones in the Middle Ages?

_____

_____

5.   Cross out the word or phrase that is **not** like the other two words or phrases. You may look up words in the glossary or in your dictionary.

a.   avoid—stay away from—try to meet

b.   valuable—useless—precious

c.   mourning—celebration—sadness

d.   ruler—follower—leader

e.   calm—fear—hysteria

2. Let's Talk!

These questions ask you about cat superstitions in your country. Talk about these questions with two or three of your classmates. After you finish talking, write your answers on the blank lines.

1.   How do people in your culture feel about cats? Are there any special superstitions regarding cats? Explain.

_____

_____

2. Do you have any special feelings about cats? If so, explain.

   _____

   _____

3. In your opinion, what is the meaning of the Chinese folktale about the cats who ruled the world and then gave up this responsibility to humans?

   _____

   _____

4. "Who knows whether the cat is not amusing herself with me more than I am with her?" Explain what this means.

   _____

   _____

   _____

3. Vocabulary Practice: Word Forms

Read each sentence carefully. Then choose the correct word form from the list, and write it on the line. (*Note:* This list has only the most common forms. It is not a complete list of all forms.) Talk about your answers with your group. **Be careful with singular/plural forms for nouns and be careful with verb tenses.**

Word Form List

	Noun	Verb	Adjective	Adverb
1.	amusement	to amuse	amusing	—
2.	preference	to prefer	preferable	—
3.	protection	to protect	protective	protectively
4.	mourning	to mourn	mournful	—
5.	ruler	to rule	—	—

1. The students liked Professor Gonsalves-Garcia because she often

    told _____ stories in class.

    You need recreation and _____ sometimes in order
    to relax.

    You _____ me when you tell those funny stories.

2. This chair is _____ to that one because it is more
    comfortable.

    Which chair do you _____?

    What is your _____ in colors?

3. The mother watched her child _____ as he played
    with the other children.

    She wanted to _____ him from danger.

    You must wear _____ gloves if you want to use
    those chemicals.

    Police are supposed to provide security and _____.

4. Her mother recently died, and she is in _____.

    She will _____ her death for a long time because
    she loved her very much.

    That song is so sad and _____.

5. Cats once _____ the world, according to a Chinese
    folktale.

    They were the _____ until they got tired of the
    responsibility.

E X P A N S I O N   A C T I V I T I E S

Interview: Superstitions

You have discussed your views on superstitions in the "Let's Talk!" exercises above. Now interview a classmate about a superstition in his or her culture. If possible, try to choose someone who comes from a different background than you do.

Planning and Conducting the Interview

A. Plan your interview. Before you interview the person, think about the questions you want to ask. Write out these questions on a piece of paper. First, try to make up your questions by yourself. Then work with a partner to get ideas for more questions. You may look back at previous units for help in developing your questions if you wish. Be sure to leave space on your paper for the answers.

B. Choose a classmate to interview.

C. Begin your interview. Do not try to write complete answers to your questions. Just make notes to help you remember the answers.

Interaction

Work with two or three other classmates. Tell the group about your interview. Tell them the name of the person you interviewed, and then tell them your questions and the answers that the person gave. Be sure to use your notes to help you remember what the person said in the interview.

Special Reading

This reading selection comes from *The Joy Luck Club,* by Amy Tan (New York: G.P. Putnam's Sons, 1989). Ms. Tan is the daughter of Chinese immigrants, and she grew up in Oakland, California. In the following passage, the Chinese-born mother is trying to explain to her American-born daughter why she must put the mirrors in just the right place in her bedroom.

"Wah!" cried the mother upon seeing the mirrored **armoire** in the **master suite** of her daughter's new **condominium**. "You cannot put mirrors at the **foot of the bed**. All your marriage happiness will **bounce** back and turn the opposite way."

"Well, that's the only place it fits, so that's where it stays," said the daughter, **irritated** that her mother saw bad omens in everything. She had heard these **warnings** all her life.

The mother frowned, reaching into her twice-used Macy's bag.[5] "Hunh, lucky I can fix it for you, then." And she pulled out the **gilt-edged** mirror she had bought at the Price Club[6] last week. It was her **housewarming present**. She leaned it against the headboard, on top of the two pillows.

"You hang it here," said the mother, pointing to the wall above. "This mirror sees that mirror—[and it will] multiply your peach-blossom luck."

"What is peach-blossom luck?"

The mother smiled, mischief in her eyes. "It is in here," she said, pointing to the mirror. "Look inside. Tell me, am I not right? In this mirror is my future grandchild, already sitting on my lap next spring."

And the daughter looked. *Haule!*[7] There it was: her own reflection looking back at her.

(190 words)

Freewriting

Write for 15 minutes about anything that comes into your mind related to this reading passage. You may want to write about a superstition or something that happened to you or to someone you know.

After you finish, read your writing to some of your classmates, and listen to their writings. Talk about the interesting points in each of the writings, and ask questions if you don't understand or if you would like to know more about something.

---

[5] **Macy's bag**—a shopping bag from Macy's, a very large department store
[6] **Price Club**—a discount store for shoppers who like to get a bargain
[7] **Haule!**—a Chinese exclamation of surprise

Quotations

Read these quotations, and explain what they mean:

"When evil recognizes itself, it destroys itself."

CHINESE SAYING FROM THE TAO

"If at first you don't succeed, try, try, try again."

PROVERB

"The third time's the charm."

PROVERB

GLOSSARY

In this glossary, words are defined according to the way they are used in the reading. Since many of these words also have other definitions, you may want to look up the words in your dictionary to get the full range of meanings. The number in parentheses refers to the page on which the word first appears in the book. For example, **accurately** is followed by (91). This means that **accurately** is first introduced on page 91.

accurately *adv.* done carefully with no errors. *Ex.* Jean finished the exam slowly but accurately. (91)

achievement *n.* accomplishment. *Ex.* Michael Jordan has had many achievements in his lifetime. (148)

actually *adv.* really; spoken in truth. *Ex.* Although she looks younger, Mary is actually 25 years old. (102)

A.D. *abbrev.* after the death of Christ. *Ex.* The Norman Conquest began in 1066 A.D. (23)

admirable *adj.* deserving of praise; excellent. *Ex.* Her efforts to walk again after the accident were truly admirable. (116)

admired *adj.* looked at with respect. *Ex.* She is an admired professor because she gets along well with both her colleagues and her students. (21)

admit *v.* to tell the truth. *Ex.* You must admit that he caused you problems. (148)

adolescence *n.* years when children become young adults. *Ex.* The years of his adolescence were painful. (92)

adorable *adj.* very cute; beautiful. *Ex.* I bought an adorable outfit for my daughter last week at the department store. (11)

advantage *n.* something good or useful. *Ex.* What are the advantages and disadvantages of attending this school? (74)

affect *v.* influence; change. *Ex.* Bad habits, such as smoking or excessive drinking, can affect your health in serious ways. (140)

afford *v.* to have enough money for something. *Ex.* Now that John has a part-time job, he can afford to go to college. (38)

almost *adv.* nearly. *Ex.* Her daughter is almost ready for school. (65)

alongside *prep.* close to; side by side with. *Ex.* She usually sits alongside me on the bus. (84)

amateur *n.* someone just beginning a sport or activity; not a professional. *Ex.* With many years of practice and a lot of hard work, an amateur can become a professional. (115)

amuse *v.* to provide enjoyment. *Ex.* The puppet show amused the children for hours. (110)

ancient *adj.* from very long ago. *Ex.* Socrates lived in ancient Greece. (123)

anthropologist *n.* a scientist who studies human culture. *Ex.* Historians, anthropologists, and archeologists have always been interested in the city of Beijing. (47)

anxiety *n.* worry; concern. *Ex.* I felt a great deal of anxiety during the final examination. (64)

application *n.* a form that you fill out to get a job, attend school, etc. *Ex.* Write your complete name on this job application. (2)

archeologist *n.* a scientist who studies objects from many years ago. *Ex.* The archeologist studied weapons, tools, and fossils to understand how people lived thousands of years ago. (47)

area *n.* region. *Ex.* Very few people live in that area of the state. (36)

argue *v.* to fight using words. *Ex.* Parents try not to argue in front of their children. (74)

armoire *n.* an upright piece of furniture placed in a bedroom and used for storing clothes. Ex. The doors of the armoire were mirrored. (162)

as opposed to *adv.* in contrast to, different from. *Ex.* He decided to buy the American car as opposed to the foreign one. (125)

at ease *adv.* calm and relaxed. *Ex.* As soon as her children were safely back at home, she felt at ease. (64)

athlete *n.* one who plays sports involving physical ability. *Ex.* Jenny is a fine athlete—she plays soccer, tennis, and golf. (36)

atmosphere *n.* what happens near or around an area. *Ex.* The current atmosphere in politics is bitter and argumentative. (118)

available *adj.* possible to have. *Ex.* Tickets for that concert are still available. (73)

average *adj.* normal. *Ex.* Charles is just an average tennis player. (37)

avoid *v.* to try not to do something. *Ex.* He avoids using the past tense in English because he does not understand it well. (139)

back and forth *adv.* moving away from and then returning back. *Ex.* When I watch a tennis game, I enjoy watching the ball go back and forth from one player to the other. (124)

baseline *n.* the end boundary of a field in sports. *Ex.* The tennis player's serve went past the baseline. (125)

be composed of *v.* to form together from different parts. *Ex.* This city is composed of many different kinds of people with different languages and customs. (71)

best *adj.* very good *(superlative)*. *Ex.* Maria is the best student in our class. (38)

betray *v.* to be disloyal or unfaithful to someone. *Ex.* Jon will never betray his wife since he loves her very much. (149)

blame *v.* to say that someone else is responsible for a wrongdoing. *Ex.* They blamed their dog for ruining the carpet, but he was innocent. (65)

bonfire *n.* a large outdoor fire. *Ex.* In 1630, the practice of burning cats in public bonfires was stopped. (157)

borough *n.* a section of New York City. *Ex.* Brooklyn is one of New York's five boroughs. (36)

bounce *v.* rebound. *Ex.* The ball bounced off the floor and broke a window. (162)

bound (to) *adj.* sure to; with certainty. *Ex.* You are bound to have fun at the picnic as long as the weather is nice and the people are friendly. (63)

break the law *v.* to commit a crime. *Ex.* If you drive while under the influence of alcohol or drugs, you are breaking the law. (21)

bury *v.* to put beneath the ground. *Ex.* He was buried near his favorite old tree. (44)

by the same token *adv.* similarly. *Ex.* Tom loves to swim; by the same token, his brother swims four times a week. (149)

calm *adj.* without excitement or worry. *Ex.* She was unusually calm before her math test. (140)

capital *n.* a city that is the center of the government. *Ex.* Mexico City is the capital of Mexico. (33)

carnival *n.* a party or celebration that anyone can go to, with music, games, etc. *Ex.* The carnival of Rio de Janeiro is famous all around the world. (110)

celebrate *v.* to mark a joyful day with special events. *Ex.* They will celebrate his birthday next week. (124)

celebration *n.* an important day. *Ex.* There are celebrations all across the United States on the Fourth of July. (108)

cemetery *n.* a place where people are buried after they die. *Ex.* People go to the cemetery to see where their relatives are buried. (156)

ceremony *n.* a special happening, such as a wedding or funeral. *Ex.* The baby received her name at a special ceremony. (12)

challenge *n.* a difficult problem or task. *Ex.* Finding a new job has been Jeanne's biggest challenge. (55)

chandelier *n.* a fixture with lights, hanging from the ceiling. *Ex.* That chandelier provides a beautiful touch to the center of the dining room. (30)

character *n.* having principles; trustworthy. *Ex.* Only people with good character will be admitted into this organization. (108)

chauffeur *n.* one who drives other people in a special car or limousine. *Ex.* Only the very rich are driven regularly by a chauffeur. (38)

chemistry *n.* the study of the nature of physical substances. *Ex.* We learned about carbon chains in the lecture on organic chemistry. (19)

circus *n.* a traveling show with animals, clowns, and other performers. *Ex.* A circus is coming to town next week. (110)

clap *v.* to put hands together to show approval. *Ex.* The audience clapped after the excellent performance. (134)

click *v.* to make a sound with the tongue. *Ex.* I could tell how nervous he was when I saw him click his tongue. (101)

coax *v.* to convince; to persuade gently. *Ex.* She coaxed him to go to the movies although he did not want to go. (101)

coincidence *n.* events that happen by chance but could seem planned. *Ex.* It was a coincidence that you decided to move to the same city as we did. (64)

collapse *v.* to fall down or in. *Ex.* The roof collapsed during the storm. (55)

colleague *n.* a fellow worker, either in business or at a university. *Ex.* Professor Walker and Dr. Gonzalez are colleagues. (101)

combination *n.* a mixture of. *Ex.* He cooked a combination of different vegetables. (54)

come up *v.* happen; occur. *Ex.* I was supposed to meet Barbara for lunch, but something came up. (63)

commercial *adj.* referring to business. *Ex.* His office is in the commercial part of the city. (36)

commit suicide *v.* to kill oneself. *Ex.* His many troubles led him to commit suicide. (92)

common *adj.* happening or found often. *Ex.* Rodriguez is a common Hispanic family name. (5)

communist *n.* a person who believes in a political and social system controlled by the government or by the people as a whole. *Ex.* The People's Republic of China is governed by communists. (46)

compete *v.* to be in a test or race in order to see who does the best. *Ex.* More than 200 runners will compete in the race. (90)

competition *n.* a contest of skill or ability. The competition begins at 8:00 tomorrow morning. (91)

competitive *adj.* See *competition*. *Ex.* In this high school, the students are very competitive. (107)

complaint *n.* negative comments made about someone or something. *Ex.* The students enjoyed this class very much and had no complaints. (91)

complicated *adj.* difficult to understand; complex. *Ex.* Understanding how to use English verb tenses is often complicated. (74)

composed See *be composed of.*

concentration *n.* paying attention carefully; thinking very hard. *Ex.* The pilot's concentration should not be interrupted. (134)

condominium *n.* an attached house or apartment that is owned rather than rented. *Ex.* She sold her condominium to a man and his daughter. (162)

confrontation *n.* coming together face to face; argument. *Ex.* They had a serious confrontation several years ago, but they are good friends today. (47)

confused *adj.* not clear; cannot understand something. *Ex.* Maria was confused about the new material that the instructor presented this week in class. (63)

connect *v.* to join together. *Ex.* This new road connects the airport and the highway. (44)

conquer *v.* to win a victory over an enemy. *Ex.* Hernando Cortes conquered the Aztecs in 1519. (54)

consumer shortage *n.* not enough food or supplies for people. *Ex.* Consumer shortages occur when food or services are not delivered to the people. (46)

contribution *n.* something that you give (along with others), usually for a good reason. *Ex.* He made a contribution to help the homeless. (73)

controversial *adj.* difficult to reach a decision; with differing points of view. *Ex.* Gun control is a controversial issue in the United States. (73)

crime *n.* something that is against the law. *Ex.* Driving under the influence of drugs or alcohol is a serious crime. (38)

criminal *n.* someone who has broken the law. *Ex.* The criminal was handcuffed by the police and then taken to the police station for questioning. (116)

critical *adj.* important; necessary. *Ex.* It is critical that you get there on time. (91)

criticize *v.* to find fault with something. *Ex.* If you criticize my work, please give me some suggestions for change. (116)

crowded *adj.* with many people. *Ex.* The subways in large cities are usually very crowded. (46)

crucify *v.* to put to death on a cross. *Ex.* Christ was crucified twenty-four hours after the Last Supper. (149)

curriculum *n.* a course of study. *Ex.* The math curriculum is very difficult. (92)

custom *n.* the usual way of doing something. *Ex.* In China, the custom is to say the family name first. (4)

customs agent *n.* a person who checks luggage when a traveler enters or leaves a foreign country. *Ex.* The customs agent will search your bags for illegal possessions. (35)

cut off *v.* to remove. *Ex.* I did not recognize my professor after he cut off his beard. (124)

damage *v.* to hurt or harm. *Ex.* The house was damaged by the fallen tree from the storm. (56)

dangerous *adj.* not safe; harmful. *Ex.* It is dangerous to allow small children to play by themselves. (38)

dare *v.* to be brave or bold enough to do something. *Ex.* I did not dare to speak English in front of the class because I was too shy and embarrassed. (101)

date *v.* to go as a couple to the movies, dinner, or entertainment. *Ex.* Liu and Fanny dated four years before they decided to get married. (11)

decade *n.* a period of ten years. *Ex.* The last decade was an important one for world peace. (90)

decline *v.* to decide not to do something. *Ex.* Mr. Jones declined the invitation to meet the President at the White House. (101)

definitely *adv.* with great certainty; without hesitation. *Ex.* When they move into their new apartment in the city, they will definitely install a burglar alarm. (28)

demand *n.* obligation; request. *Ex.* There are unusual demands being placed on me at this job. (47)

demand *v.* to ask for. *Ex.* The workers went on strike for a week because they demanded a new contract and did not get one. (47)

democracy *n.* a government in which the people elect officials. *Ex.* In a democracy, people vote for the president. (70)

democratic *adj.* See *democracy*. *Ex.* The United States has a democratic form of government. (47)

demonstrate *v.* to show or display. *Ex.* The students demonstrated how well they understood the lesson when they did well on the exam. (116)

demonstration *n.* a public display of disapproval of something—for example, of the government or an important issue. *Ex.* There are often demonstrations in countries that have unstable governments. (47)

deny *v.* to say that something is not true. *Ex.* Lillian often denies how intelligent she is, but everyone knows the truth. (116)

depart *v.* to leave. *Ex.* Their train departs from the station at 6:30. (147)

depend *v.* to need; to use for help. *Ex.* He depends upon his parents to pay for his education. (36)

deserve *v.* to be worthy of something. *Ex.* The Smith family worked very hard to buy their home, and they certainly deserve it. (109)

destroy *v.* to break in pieces; to ruin completely. *Ex.* The earthquake destroyed many parts of the city. (54)

devote *v.* to give a lot of time or money to something. *Ex.* Sigmund Freud devoted his life to the study of psychoanalysis. (109)

disappointed *adj.* sad that something did not happen. *Ex.* She was disappointed when the letter did not arrive. (107)

discouraged *adj.* losing confidence and desire. *Ex.* Don't be discouraged; try again. (73)

disguise *n.* a way to change one's appearance. *Ex.* He did not want to be recognized when he appeared on television, so he wore a disguise. (157)

distorted *adj.* to be twisted out of shape. *Ex.* The sweater was so distorted after it was washed that I was not sure if I could wear it anymore. (140)

district *n.* a particular area in a city, town, or country. *Ex.* Let's walk around the theater district this afternoon. (36)

dominate *v.* to have control over someone or something. *Ex.* China and the Four Tigers are expected to dominate economic development in the Pacific Rim in years to come. (90)

drag *v.* to pull along on the ground or floor. *Ex.* The car dragged the man for 20 feet before it came to a stop. (141)

draw *v.* produce effect with some effort. *Ex.* Mike is so talkative that he is able to draw out even the quietest person. (140)

drop out *v.* to leave before something is finished. *Ex.* He dropped out of high school last year. (73)

earthquake *n.* a sudden strong shaking of the ground. *Ex.* The earthquake destroyed 45 homes and 20 businesses. (55)

effect *n.* result; something that happens because of something else. *Ex.* This medicine has a bad effect on my stomach. (83)

elect *v.* to select for a political office. *Ex.* I am going to vote next week to elect a new president. (44)

elevation *n.* the height above sea level. *Ex.* This town's elevation is approximately 1,000 feet above sea level. (53)

embalm *v.* to preserve a dead body with chemicals. *Ex.* The body was embalmed before it was buried. (156)

embarrassed *adj.* feeling ashamed or uncomfortable. *Ex.* The boy was embarrassed when his parents kissed him in front of his friends. (65)

encouragement *n.* support; being given the confidence to do something. *Ex.* I was lucky to receive my parents' encouragement throughout my school years. (108)

enemy *n.* someone or something that hates or fights another person or country. *Ex.* During World War II, Germany and the United States were enemies. (124)

enforcement *n.* the carrying out of a rule or law. *Ex.* Once Juan receives his degree in political science, he will pursue a career in law enforcement. (72)

entertainment *n.* a party, show, concert, sports event, or other activity that people enjoy. *Ex.* What type of entertainment do you like the most? (108)

environment *n.* the air, land, and water surrounding where people live. *Ex.* One of the ways in which I protect the environment is by recycling paper, glass, plastic, and aluminum. (55)

establish *v.* to begin; to start up. *Ex.* The leaders established a new government. (81)

event *n.* one activity in a sports program. *Ex.* The first event is the 100-meter race. (118)

evidence *n.* proof that something happened. *Ex.* What evidence do you have that Mr. Watson actually stole money from his company? (124)

evil *n.* a hostile force; the opposite of *good*. *Ex.* In the movie, the hero fought the forces of evil. (148)

excellent *adj.* very good. *Ex.* He studied hard and received an excellent grade on the test. (44)

exception *n.* a case that is different from the rest. *Ex.* I usually do not go out to the movies on a weekday evening, but tonight is an exception. (84)

excited *adj.* very happy about something. *Ex.* She is excited that her parents are coming to visit her from Colombia. (107)

exhibit *n.* something that is shown in public. *Ex.* There is an exhibit of antique automobiles at the Transportation Museum this weekend. (124)

exist *v.* to be available. *Ex.* Did this type of book exist a century ago? (37)

expensive *adj.* costing a lot of money. *Ex.* A Rolls Royce is a very expensive automobile. (38)

explore *v.* to look around; to search while traveling. *Ex.* She is exploring her options in the field of social work. (72)

export *n.* goods made in one country to be sold in another country. *Ex.* The United States has many exports. (90)

export *v.* to send things out of one country for sale to other countries. *Ex.* India exports clothing to many countries. (80)

extraordinary *adj.* more than what is common. *Ex.* Due to his extraordinary musical talent, Roberto was playing piano before a large audience at the age of 10. (90)

extremely *adv.* very. *Ex.* Parts of the U.S. have extremely cold weather in the winter. (53)

factory *n.* a place where things are made. *Ex.* The rubber factory produces a terrible odor that local residents can detect on a windy day. (54)

failure *n.* having no success. *Ex.* His new business was a failure. (92)

fairy *n.* an imaginary figure that looks human. *Ex.* Do you believe in the tooth fairy? (139)

fall apart *v.* to break into several or many pieces. *Ex.* You need to follow the washing instructions on that garment carefully so that it does not fall apart. (133)

famous *adj.* known by many people. *Ex.* The state of California is famous for its wine. (36)

fancy *adj.* with special decoration. *Ex.* Are you wearing a fancy dress to the dance? (30)

fascinating *adj.* very interesting. *Ex.* I think the history of Japan is fascinating. (54)

fashion *n.* a popular custom or style. *Ex.* She always wears the latest fashions. (22)

fate *n.* what will happen in the future; destiny. *Ex.* Is it fate that I ended up marrying you? (142)

fear *v.* to be afraid of. *Ex.* Rami feared the dark because of a bad experience he had as a child. (83)

fear (of) *n.* See *fear. Ex.* It is not uncommon for a student at a prestigious university to commit suicide due to a fear of failure. (92)

federal *adj.* having to do with the national government. *Ex.* Public schooling in the U.S. is paid for by the local, state, and federal governments. (70)

fertility *n.* the ability to reproduce. *Ex.* Couples who cannot have children go to special doctors who deal with problems of fertility. (124)

festival *n.* a party or celebration for a special reason, usually at the same time every year. *Ex.* There is a festival in that school every spring. (108)

figure out *v.* to learn how to do something. *Ex.* It took the foreign tourists several weeks to figure out the public transportation system in the city. (64)

fill out *v.* to write information on a form completely. *Ex.* Before getting accepted into any university, you need to fill out an application form. (2)

finance *n.* the study of money and how it is controlled in business. *Ex.* In college, he hopes to major in finance and eventually get an MBA. (37)

financial aid *n.* money to help pay for school. *Ex.* She received some financial aid from the college. (38)

fit *v.* to be suited for. *Ex.* The colorful clothes that she is wearing fit her personality. (11)

focus *v.* to look carefully in one direction. *Ex.* Pedro is focusing on his studies this semester because he wants to graduate in May. (142)

folklore commission *n.* a group of people who try to keep alive the traditions of their country. *Ex.* The Irish Folklore Commission is committed to preserving the habits and beliefs of Ireland and its people. (139)

foot of the bed *n.* *(idiom)* the end of the bed where one's feet usually rest. *Ex.* In the winter, I often keep a blanket by the foot of the bed in case my legs get cold. (162)

forbidding *adj.* dangerous. *Ex.* The fires rushing through Southern California were accompanied by forbidding winds. (64)

force *n.* power; strong entity. *Ex.* A hurricane is a powerful force. (133)

foreign *adj.* from a different country. *Ex.* In China, you can now buy foreign goods, although things were different years ago. (46)

foretell *v.* to tell about what will happen in the future. *Ex.* Can anyone foretell what will happen 100 years from now? (142)

form *n.* a type of. *Ex.* Tae Kwon Do is the Korean form of karate. (108)

former *adj.* previous. *Ex.* Who are your current and former employers? (90)

fortune *n.* luck. *Ex.* In the 1st century B.C., the Romans believed that people's health and fortune changed every seven years. (141)

friend *n.* an acquaintance who feels positively toward one. *Ex.* Robert is my best friend. (56)

frighten *v.* to scare. *Ex.* Were you frightened by the storm last night? (141)

fulfill *v.* to meet expectations. *Ex.* Before taking courses in your major, you need to fulfill all your other college requirements. (91)

gable *n.* the three-cornered upper end of a wall where it meets a roof. *Ex.* Mirrors were placed on the gables of Chinese houses to scare away evil spirits. (141)

gender *n.* which sex a person is: male or female. *Ex.* Some South American schools still separate students by gender. (82)

gesture *n.* hand movements that have certain meanings. *Ex.* Gestures in one culture might have an entirely different meaning in another culture. (116)

ghost *n.* the spirit of a dead person. *Ex.* Do you think that there are any ghosts in this house? (140)

gift *n.* a present. *Ex.* What kind of gift would a five-year-old girl enjoy? (109)

gilt-edged *adj.* having a shiny metal covering on the outside. *Ex.* He displayed his gilt-edged sword in front of the crowd. (162)

give up *v.* to stop doing something after trying very hard to succeed. *Ex.* After playing piano for eight years, Junko decided to give it up. (133)

glamorous *adj.* having special charm and beauty. *Ex.* Marilyn Monroe was a very glamorous actress. (20)

goal *n.* something a person want to accomplish or achieve. *Ex.* One of my goals in life is to travel around the world. (124)

goalpost *n.* In American football, one of two vertical bars that mark the goal. *Ex.* The player kicked the ball straight through the goalposts. (134)

god *n.* any being that people think has power over them and nature. *Ex.* The gods of ancient Greece and Rome were very powerful. (140)

good luck *n.* positive fortune. *Ex.* Ruth wished me good luck on my exam. (13)

graduate *v.* to complete a school program. *Ex.* He will graduate from high school next spring. (82)

grief *n.* a feeling of loss due to the death of a loved one. *Ex.* It is hard to know what to say to someone who is overcome with grief. (156)

group project *n.* an activity in which students work together. *Ex.* The professor assigns a group project to our class toward the end of each unit. (71)

guest worker *n.* a foreigner who comes to another country for work. *Ex.* Germany accepts guest workers from Eastern Europe. (82)

hang in there *expr.* to continue with what one is doing. *Ex.* I almost quit school, but my parents told me to hang in there. (134)

harm *v.* to hurt. *Ex.* Although the baby fell out of his crib, he was not severely harmed. (156)

harsh *adj.* very strong. *Ex.* If you use such harsh words at the interview, I do not believe that you will ever be considered for the job. (149)

healing *adj.* causing to improve someone's health. *Ex.* Herbal teas often have healing powers. (151)

healthy *adj.* without sickness. *Ex.* You can try to live a healthy life by eating right, getting exercise, and getting good medical care. (108)

historian *n.* one who studies the events of the past. *Ex.* Historians are interested in world wars. (47)

homeless *adj.* without a place to live. *Ex.* We felt sorry for the poor homeless person. (38)

honor *n.* a sign of respect. *Ex.* The statue was erected in honor of Dr. Martin Luther King, Jr. (12)

horrified *adj.* surprised about a shocking event. *Ex.* I was horrified to hear that the shooting took place in my friends' apartment building. (64)

hourglass *n.* A time-measuring instrument in which a certain amount of sand or other substance flows from the upper chamber into the lower one. *Ex.* My aunt collects old hourglasses and uses them to time her cooking. (134)

housewarming present *n.* a gift for a new home. *Ex.* For a housewarming present, I brought my friends a coffeemaker. (162)

housing *n.* places where people live. *Ex.* A city contains many kinds of housing: apartments, houses, and hotels, among others. (47)

huge *adj.* very large. *Ex.* After Mr. Smith earned a lot of money in the stock market, he bought a huge house in a beautiful town. (47)

hysteria *n.* uncontrollable reaction to something, such as laughing and crying. *Ex.* When fear and hysteria about witches grew in the Middle Ages, people began to fear black cats. (157)

image *n.* picture of someone or something in the mind. *Ex.* The governor will have to strengthen his image if he wants to be reelected. (140)

imitate *v.* to do the same thing as someone else. *Ex.* Children often imitate whatever their friends do in order to be accepted by them. (116)

impressive *adj.* causing admiration because of quality or size. *Ex.* The President gave an impressive speech on television last night. (148)

include *v.* to count something as part of the total. *Ex.* The professor included Mars in his lecture on the planets. (90)

indignantly *adv.* with feelings of anger. *Ex.* He indignantly walked away after being laid off from his job. (139)

inflation *n.* the rate of increase of prices. *Ex.* Inflation was 7% last year. (46)

influence *v.* to have an effect on. *Ex.* My education has positively influenced my life. (108)

ingredient *n.* one of the parts of a mixture. *Ex.* The main ingredient in bread is flour. (150)

inherit *v.* to receive something, especially from someone who has died. *Ex.* When my grandmother died, I inherited some antique jewelry. (30)

injure *v.* to harm or hurt. *Ex.* Fortunately, nobody was injured in the car accident. (56)

innocent *adj.* not responsible for a crime. *Ex.* The jury had to decide whether the man was innocent or guilty. (149)

in shape See *shape.*

instead of *adv.* in place of something. *Ex.* Instead of cooking tonight, let's go out to dinner. (71)

invade *v.* to enter a country and attack it. *Ex.* Germany invaded Poland in 1939. (54)

invisible *adj.* not possible to be seen. *Ex.* Carbon monoxide is a dangerous, invisible gas. (140)

irritated *adj.* annoyed. *Ex.* Please don't get irritated with me if I ask you to take out the garbage. (162)

issue *n.* a problem for discussion. *Ex.* Bilingual education is an important issue in American education. (74)

joke *v.* to say something funny. *Ex.* Marian joked with George about his haircut, but he did not think it was funny. (64)

kid *n.* a child. *Ex.* I promised to take my kids to the aquarium today. (117)

Koran *n.* a holy book for Muslims. *Ex.* He read to us from the Koran. (13)

largest *adj.* greatest in size. *Ex.* The largest lecture class in this university is Introduction to Psychology. (36)

lecture *n.* a talk that teaches something. *Ex.* The professor gave an interesting lecture. (83)

lie *n.* not the truth. *Ex.* Children often tell lies in order to get attention. (30)

limited *adj.* having rules about who can be part of something. *Ex.* This race is limited to children seven years old or younger. (74)

limousine *n.* an expensive car operated by a paid driver. *Ex.* The chief executive officer was driven to the airport in a limousine. (38)

literate *adj.* able to read and write. *Ex.* Yu is literate in both Chinese and English. (90)

located *adj.* situated; where something can be found. *Ex.* New Hampshire is located between Vermont and Maine. (44)

logically *adv.* having good sense and reasoning. *Ex.* When you study for an exam, besides memorizing details, you must also try to think logically. (92)

lowered *adj.* in a softer manner. *Ex.* The mother used a lowered voice when she wanted the baby to fall asleep. (139)

luck *n.* chance; good or bad fortune. *Ex.* Some people think a black cat brings bad luck. (124)

luxury *adj.* very expensive. *Ex.* There are new luxury homes being built nearby, but I do not think I will be able to afford one. (148)

magically *adv.* performed with strange or special powers. *Ex.* During the storm last Tuesday, the sun magically appeared and the rain stopped. (108)

mainland *n.* land mass, not including islands. *Ex.* Parts of Cape Cod are not connected to the mainland. (36)

maintain *v.* to continue as before. *Ex.* Puerto Rico would like to maintain its status as a commonwealth of the United States. (83)

man of letters *n.* one who produces and studies literature. *Ex.* William Faulkner was a noted man of letters. (139)

manuscript *n.* the version of a book before it is printed. *Ex.* The author wrote many versions of the manuscript before the company published it. (156)

master suite *n.* a bedroom with an attached bathroom. *Ex.* Most small houses do not have a master suite. (162)

material *adj.* concerning things. *Ex.* Money can bring material success, but not happiness. (70)

memorize *v.* to learn something word for word. *Ex.* I have to memorize a poem for English class. (80)

mention *v.* to discuss briefly. *Ex.* You mentioned that there will be a meeting tomorrow night, but I do not believe you told me the time or place. (156)

merchandise *n.* things that people can purchase at a store. *Ex.* That department store has beautiful merchandise. (46)

midst *n.* at the same time as. *Ex.* It is surprising that in the midst of technological advancements, superstitions still exist. (148)

miniskirt *n.* a very small women's skirt reaching only to the middle of the thigh. *Ex.* In the 1960s, miniskirts were very popular. (46)

mock *adj.* in an imitating fashion. *Ex.* His brother clicked his tongue in mock disapproval and teased him because of the romantic story he told. (101)

model *n.* a method of doing something that is followed by others. *Ex.* If you are not sure about how to do this exercise, look at the model on page 134. (71)

modern *adj.* relating to the present. *Ex.* In Egypt, you can see buildings from both modern and ancient times. (81)

motivate *v.* to encourage to work harder. *Ex.* Good teachers motivate their students and do not discourage them when they make mistakes. (91)

mourn *v.* to feel grief (due to the death of a loved one). *Ex.* The widow mourned her husband until she died. (156)

multiple-choice exam *n.* a test wherein students select the correct answer from several possible choices given. *Ex.* Rather than an essay text, the instructor decided to give a multiple-choice exam. (91)

name after *v.* to give a baby the same name as another person. *Ex.* My daughter is named after her great-grandmother. (11)

namesake *n.* a person given the name of someone. *Ex.* John F. Kennedy, Jr. was his father's namesake. (12)

nervously *adv.* with worry and concern. *Ex.* I looked nervously at my exam results, but I saw that I had passed. (63)

Never mind! *exp.* to tell someone to stop doing what he or she is doing. *Ex.* Never mind! I don't really need your help after all. (35)

nod *v.* to indicate "yes" by moving one's head downward. *Ex.* When I asked her to go to the movies, she nodded and said, "Sure, that sounds great." (134)

noted (for) *adj.* famous. *Ex.* Michael Jordan is noted for his basketball skills. (54)

nude *adj.* having no clothes on. *Ex.* Nude sunbathing is acceptable on beaches in France. (109)

obscene *adj.* nasty; words and actions considered unacceptable. *Ex.* In a competitive sports match, the players occasionally use obscene language. (116)

occur *v.* to happen. *Ex.* I don't remember where the accident occurred. (118)

offer *v.* to try to give to someone. *Ex.* He offered to pay five hundred dollars for the ring, but I believe it is worth more. (37)

omen *n.* a feeling or sign about what will happen in the future. *Ex.* Having had trouble with his car, Eduardo considered it a good omen when the car started. (141)

openness *n.* a political situation creating more opportunities for people. *Ex.* People in China were not sure how much openness they really wanted. (47)

opposed See *as opposed to.*

opposing *adj.* on the other side. *Ex.* The opposing team is from Portugal. (125)

orderly *adj.* following closely to the rules. *Ex.* A more orderly game calls for both sides to start at the same time. (125)

originally *adv.* from the beginning. *Ex.* Originally, he wanted to vote for the Republican, but he decided to vote for the Democrat at the last minute. (148)

outcome *n.* result. *Ex.* What was the outcome of the tennis match? (108)

outstanding *adj.* excellent. *Ex.* His presentation on computers was outstanding. (93)

pagan *n.* one who believes in a primitive religion or none at all. *Ex.* The missionary saw the natives as pagans. (149)

pal *n.* friend. *Ex.* He and his pals are going out to celebrate tonight. (133)

participate *v.* to be part of something. *Ex.* Everyone in the class participated in the game. (108)

passion *n.* love. *Ex.* He has a great passion for classical music. (90)

peace *n.* without war. *Ex.* He hopes that in his lifetime there will be peace in every region of the world. (110)

peaceful *adj.* without conflict or war; quiet. *Ex.* The government meetings were very peaceful this year. (108)

perform *v.* to put on a show—e.g., music, dance, or a play. *Ex.* The students will perform before an audience in their school at the end of the year. (109)

period *n.* length; measure. *Ex.* Learning chemistry requires an extended period of study. (73)

pet *n.* an animal kept in or near the home and enjoyed by the family. *Ex.* When I was growing up, we never had pets however, we now have a cat and a dog. (156)

point *n.* characteristics; qualities. *Ex.* There are both negative and positive points regarding the President's proposed health-care bill. (84)

point out *v.* to show or indicate. *Ex.* The weatherman has pointed out that there is going to be a big storm coming our way this weekend. (74)

pond *n.* a small lake. *Ex.* In this part of the country, there are many beautiful ponds and streams. (140)

population *n.* the number of people in a city, state, country, etc. *Ex.* What is the population of your native country? (36)

positive *adj.* good; favorable. *Ex.* She received many positive comments on her oral report. (84)

possession *n.* a thing that one owns. *Ex.* Our car is one of our most important possessions. (70)

power *n.* ability to do something; strength. *Ex.* Many people do not like the power of our government. (36)

praise *v.* to honor. *Ex.* Anna's guitar teacher praised her on her progress. (109)

preach *v.* to say in order to change people's minds. *Ex.* You should remember to practice what you preach. (156)

precious *adj.* very valuable. *Ex.* Diamonds are possibly the most precious gems in the world. (155)

pressure *n.* a weight or force. *Ex.* He is under a lot of pressure to pass the exam. (91)

pretend *v.* act as if something is true. *Ex.* The boys pretended to be pirates. (139)

prevent *v.* to stop something from happening. *Ex.* What can you do to prevent a cold? (110)

pride *n.* satisfaction. *Ex.* Lawrence felt the pride of being a winner. (108)

primitive *adj.* relating to early stages of civilization. *Ex.* Anthropologists study about primitive people and the tools they used. (123)

private life *n.* time spent out of the public's attention. *Ex.* Ever since Mel Gibson became a star, he has tried to keep his private life separate from his professional life. (116)

privilege *n.* a special thing that not everybody can have. *Ex.* I think it is a privilege to be a part of this group. (109)

produce *v.* to make something. *Ex.* That factory produces tires. (71)

producer *n.* a person or thing that makes something. *Ex.* Japan is an important producer of computers. (80)

professional *adj.* playing sports for money. *Ex.* Professional athletes could not compete in the Olympics until recently. (37)

promote *v.* to help something start and continue. *Ex.* This group promotes equal education for all. (110)

prosperity *n.* wealth. *Ex.* She achieved prosperity due to the wise investments she made in the stock market. (124)

protect *v.* not to let harm occur to something or someone. *Ex.* To protect his family, he installed a smoke detector in his home. (55)

provincial *adj.* old-fashioned; simple. *Ex.* Alan's provincial ideas on male and female roles in a relationship caused his girlfriend to break up with him. (63)

pursue *v.* to try to achieve a certain goal. *Ex.* Mary wanted to pursue a career in medicine, but in college she decided she was not very interested in science. (72)

push *v.* to use one's hands to move something in a different direction. *Ex.* As hard as the firefighter pushed, she could not open the door to the burning house. (118)

put to death *v.* to kill someone by execution. *Ex.* He was put to death because of the crime he committed. (156)

range *n.* wide variety. *Ex.* This school offers a range of courses, from liberal arts to engineering. (72)

rapidly *adv.* quickly. *Ex.* Because the teacher went over the material rapidly, I did not understand it very well. (82)

ray *n.* a beam of light. *Ex.* The rays of the sun are strongest in the summer. (142)

recent *adj.* relating to the current time. *Ex.* Have any wars been fought in your country in recent history? (71)

record *n.* accomplishment. *Ex.* He set a new record for the most points in one game. (93)

reed *n.* a thin piece of wood. *Ex.* Have you ever played a musical instrument with a reed in the mouthpiece? (124)

reflection *n.* a picture of oneself in a mirror or water surface. *Ex.* He was able to see his reflection in the pond. (140)

reform *v.* a change to make a situation better. *Ex.* The President is currently trying to reform the health-care system in the United States. (92)

region *n.* a geographical area. *Ex.* Which region of France produces the best wine? (90)

relate to *v.* to have a connection with something. *Ex.* How does the material in this course relate to what will appear on the exam? (72)

relative *n.* people in one's family, including grandparents, aunts, uncles, and cousins. *Ex.* My relatives are coming to visit us for Thanksgiving. (56)

relaxing *adj.* having a calming and soothing effect. *Ex.* Since I have been very busy at work lately, I am looking forward to a relaxing vacation. (108)

relief *n.* feeling that a situation has improved after thinking something worse could have happened. *Ex.* She breathed a sigh of relief once her daughter returned home safely from the party. (63)

relieved *adj.* See *relief. Ex.* They were relieved to find out that they did not owe the government any money. (64)

renew *v.* to apply for something again. *Ex.* You need to renew your driver's license every four years. (2)

report *v.* to tell or write a story about something. *Ex.* The newspaper reported on the death of the actor. (55)

requirement *n.* something that is necessary to complete before doing another thing. *Ex.* What are the requirements for becoming an electrician in this state? (72)

rescue *adj.* regarding an act that saves someone or something from danger. *Ex.* Many people helped with the rescue attempt. (56)

reservation *n.* an arrangement to have something in advance. *Ex.* I have a reservation for the 5:00 P.M. train to Boston for next Friday. (147)

resignation *n.* accepting something without complaining. *Ex.* He accepted the difficult assignment with resignation. (101)

resources *n.* a supply of something. *Ex.* Do you have enough financial resources to invest in a college education for your children? (92)

respect *v.* admiring someone for his or her good qualities. *Ex.* Do you respect your boss? (12)

respond *v.* to react to a situation by doing something. *Ex.* After the big fight we had last night, my husband responded today by sending me flowers. (47)

restriction *n.* a rule; something that limits. *Ex.* There are very few restrictions on travel in the United States. (13)

result *n.* the end of something. *Ex.* What was the result of the trial? (74)

ridiculous *adj.* crazy; not common. *Ex.* At first the idea sounded ridiculous, but after discussing it for a while we realized it was a very good one. (140)

rite *n.* a religious custom. *Ex.* Which rites are part of your religious tradition? (140)

role *n.* a part to play; a function to carry out. *Ex.* What is a teacher's role outside the classroom? (80)

role model *n.* a person admired by others because of the excellent job he or she does. *Ex.* Nolan Ryan is a role model for many young people today. (109)

roof *n.* the top of a house or building. *Ex.* The old roof collapsed because of the strong winds from the storm last night. (30)

rough *adj.* dangerous. *Ex.* Being a firefighter is rough. (125)

rubble *n.* broken stones or bricks. *Ex.* After the earthquake, all that was left of our building was rubble. (55)

run-down *adj.* in poor condition. *Ex.* All the run-down houses on this street were destroyed. (38)

rush hour *n.* busy times in morning and evening traffic. *Ex.* If you get to work before or after rush hour, your commute will be quicker. (46)

sack *n.* a bag. *Ex.* She brought home a sack of potatoes from the store. (30)

sad *adj.* not happy. *Ex.* She was sad to hear the news of the layoffs at the factory. (107)

safer *adj.* more secure; less dangerous. *Ex.* In my opinion, traveling by car is safer than going by plane. (125)

saying *n.* a sentence that teaches a moral or lesson. *Ex.* There is a similar saying in my language: "Don't count your chickens before they're hatched." (119)

scare away *v.* to cause someone to leave because of fear. *Ex.* The difficult exam at the beginning of the course scared away some of the students. (141)

schedule *v.* to arrange according to time. *Ex.* It's important to schedule an appointment for a haircut before you go there. (148)

scream *n.* a loud cry of fear or pain. *Ex.* A scream was coming from the burning building. (55)

search *v.* to look for. *Ex.* She searched all over for her glasses, but she couldn't find them anywhere. (63)

secure *adj.* safe. *Ex.* Maria feels secure once she arrives home and locks her door. (44)

seer *n.* someone who can foretell the future. *Ex.* She asked a seer about what will happen to her in the future. (140)

segregated *adj.* separated by sex or race. *Ex.* Classrooms in the United States are not segregated by sex as they are in Saudi Arabia. (82)

setting *n.* a place where something happens. *Ex.* The setting of the movie is Los Angeles. (53)

shaman *n.* a medicine man or magician. *Ex.* The tribe's shaman tried to cure illness with magic spells. (151)

shape *n.* good physical condition. *Ex.* Now that Jane exercises four times a week, she is in shape. (108)

shave off *v.* to cut facial hair with a razor. *Ex.* Have you ever wondered how you would look if you shaved off your beard? (156)

sheepishly *adv.* with some embarrassment and fear. *Ex.* She sheepishly walked away when she realized that she had made a mistake. (102)

shift *n.* a change from one to another. *Ex.* There was a shift from a conservative mayor to a more liberal one in this city. (110)

shiver *v.* to shake because of cold temperature. *Ex.* After playing out in the snow for a few hours, the children began to shiver. (133)

shocking *adj.* causing an unpleasant surprise. *Ex.* The news of his death was shocking. (56)

shove *v.* to push someone hard. *Ex.* During the fight, the boys pushed and shoved each other, and then walked away angrily. (118)

Shrove Tuesday *n.* a holiday celebrated in England during the Middle Ages. *Ex.* People once played an ancient form of football on Shrove Tuesday. (125)

shrug *v.* to raise one's shoulders to show doubt. *Ex.* He shrugged his shoulders when I asked him a question that he was not able to answer. (101)

shy *adj.* uncomfortable with talking to others in public. *Ex.* Their daughter is very shy and has a difficult time playing with other children. (101)

similar *adj.* almost or somewhat the same as. *Ex.* Baseball is similar to cricket. (124)

simple *adj.* easy; not complicated. *Ex.* When I studied math in school, I felt that algebra was simple but that geometry was difficult. (71)

single *adj.* one only. *Ex.* I'd like a single serving, please. (64)

site *n.* place. *Ex.* What is the exact site of the house? (54)

skill *n.* an ability to do something well. *Ex.* Using a computer is one of her skills. (116)

skyscraper *n.* a very tall building. *Ex.* There are many skyscrapers in downtown Los Angeles. (36)

slave *n.* a worker owned by another person. *Ex.* Many countries used to have slaves. (109)

snap *v.* to react with a harsh response. *Ex.* Because Sue was in a bad mood, she snapped at me when I asked her a simple question. (63)

so long *expr.* to say good-bye to someone. *Ex.* At the airport, Maria's family waved to her, and she said, "So long, everyone!" (134)

sob *v.* to cry. *Ex.* The child sobbed for hours when his parents left him with a babysitter. (30)

soul *n.* the part of someone that is believed to stay alive after death. *Ex.* Although he died, his soul lived on forever. (140)

specialty *n.* a type of food that is popular for its good quality. *Ex.* This restaurant serves specialties from Greece and Southern Italy. (37)

spectator *n.* a person who watches. *Ex.* Thousands of spectators came to the game. (108)

spirit *n.* the feeling and soul inside of someone. *Ex.* His body was weak from his illness, but his spirit and commitment to recovering were strong. (110)

spirits *n.* ghosts; supernatural beings. *Ex.* He could not see the spirits, but he could feel their power. (141)

split up *v.* to separate; to get divorced. *Ex.* When parents split up, the children often remain with their mother. (133)

sportsmanship *n.* the way in which athletes conduct themselves during a game. *Ex.* They displayed good sportsmanship when they shook hands with the losers after the game. (116)

square *adj.* with four sides of equal length. *Ex.* Is your kitchen table square or round? (36)

stamp *v.* to put an official seal on a document. *Ex.* Once the customs officer stamped the passport, the tourist was allowed to return home. (35)

standards *n.* expectations of quality. *Ex.* This restaurant has very high standards. (74)

stipend *n.* an amount of money to supplement income. *Ex.* In addition to free tuition, Liu received a stipend to cover additional expenses. (82)

stock exchange *n.* a place where parts of companies are bought and sold on an open market. *Ex.* The New York Stock Exchange is on Wall Street. (37)

story *n.* a floor in a building. *Ex.* That building is 50 stories high. (36)

strange *adj.* unusual; uncommon. *Ex.* That movie was very strange. (140)

straw *n.* dried grain that is used to make baskets or mats. *Ex.* Wicker baskets are made of straw. (124)

strike *v.* to hit. *Ex.* A hurricane struck the town during the night. (55)

struggle *n.* a difficult situation. *Ex.* Teenagers often have a power struggle with their parents. (148)

stuck *adj.* unable to move from a situation. *Ex.* If you drop out of high school, you will be stuck working in low-paying jobs for the rest of your life. (133)

substitute *n.* someone who takes the place of another. *Ex.* When Mr. Smith needed surgery, a substitute was hired until he returned to school. (108)

superstition *n.* a belief held in magic or chance. *Ex.* Do you believe in any superstitions? (140)

support *v.* to uphold; to back up. *Ex.* We supported our local baseball team. (109)

supposed *adj.* probable; likely to happen. *Ex.* It is supposed to rain this afternoon. (63)

surprise *n.* an unexpected event. *Ex.* It was a big surprise to see Mark after so many years. (11)

surprise *v.* See *surprise (n.)*. *Ex.* It surprises me that there are so many rich and poor people in the same city. (38)

surround *v.* to go around all sides. *Ex.* The police surrounded the building. (44)

survive *v.* to continue to live. *Ex.* All four passengers survived the car crash. (27)

swear *v.* to use harsh words to someone. *Ex.* It is impolite for athletes and fans to swear at each other during a game. (116)

syllable *n.* the part of a word containing a vowel sound. *Ex.* How many syllables are there in the word *realize*? (30)

symbol *n.* a sign or object that represents something. *Ex.* These jade earrings are my good-luck symbol. (124)

taste *n.* what one likes and dislikes. *Ex.* She has good taste in music. (36)

taxes *n.* money paid to the government for services. *Ex.* How much money do you pay in income taxes? (109)

taxi *n.* a vehicle that people hire to take them to a destination. *Ex.* In New York City, many people travel by taxi. (46)

tease *v.* to make jokes about someone. *Ex.* The children teased the little girl because she wore glasses. (101)

technological *adj.* pertaining to the study and use of scientific ideas to make things. *Ex.* Technological advances allow many people to live comfortably today. (81)

temperate *adj.* not too hot or cold. *Ex.* San Francisco has a temperate climate. (53)

territory *n.* an area of land owned by a certain group. *Ex.* The territory along the French border was once occupied by the Germans. (125)

theme *n.* a topic. *Ex.* What theme will be addressed in this lecture? (72)

thick *adj.* congested. *Ex.* The bean soup was very thick. (30)

tiny *adj.* very small. *Ex.* Have you ever seen Mike's tiny dog? (63)

tomb *n.* a grave. *Ex.* Who is buried in that tomb? (156)

ton *n.* 2,000 pounds; a large amount. *Ex.* After the earthquake, tons of rock covered the city. (55)

tourist *n.* a person who travels somewhere on vacation. *Ex.* There were many German tourists in Italy when we were there last year. (35)

trading *n.* business of buying and selling goods. *Ex.* Trading is often seen in cities with active ports. (44)

traditional *adj.* done the same way for many years. *Ex.* This rug has a traditional design. (13)

tragedy *n.* a very sad happening. *Ex.* The earthquake was horrible; many people died in the tragedy. (118)

tragic *adj.* very sad. *Ex.* Did you see the tragic story on the news last night? (47)

trinity *n.* in Christianity, consisting of the Father, the Son, and the Holy Ghost. *Ex.* The congregation prayed to the holy trinity. (151)

turmoil *n.* having confusion and problems. *Ex.* The superstition about the number 13 goes back to Loki, the god of evil and turmoil. (148)

tutoring *n.* extra help with learning a subject. *Ex.* Johnny was not able to read well, so his parents hired someone to help with his tutoring. (73)

typical *adj.* common. *Ex.* What is the typical cost of a four-year college education? (37)

uglier *adj.* not as beautiful as. *Ex.* This dog is uglier than that one. (30)

uncertain *adj.* not sure. *Ex.* He is uncertain about whether he can attend the meeting next week in Washington. (108)

undertake *v.* to begin. *Ex.* The managers first wanted the employees to undertake the year-end project, but they decided to do it themselves. (148)

unfortunately *adv.* sadly; unluckily. *Ex.* Unfortunately, people do not always help other people. (63)

uniform *n.* special clothing worn for a job or school. *Ex.* During the years George went to private school, he had to wear a uniform. (46)

unusual *adj.* not common; strange. *Ex.* Last night, I saw a very unusual movie. (20)

uphold *v.* to support. *Ex.* When you become a lawyer, you pledge to uphold the laws of the land. (140)

upset *v.* to make someone sad or disappointed. *Ex.* That they were not able to meet her at the airport upset her. (134)

useful *adj.* having a purpose. *Ex.* I decided to get you a useful gift rather than a decorative one. (38)

value *n.* importance; worth. *Ex.* A smart shopper always looks for good value. (91)

values *n.* people's ideas about how important something is. *Ex.* Their choice of a high-quality school district reflects their educational values. (70)

vary *v.* to change. *Ex.* Climates tend to vary from region to region. (74)

version *n.* a way of doing something. *Ex.* Today's American football is a version of ancient Greek football. (125)

victory *n.* winning a battle, race, or struggle. *Ex.* The winning team celebrated their victory the entire evening. (124)

violence *n.* force that causes injury. *Ex.* Fighting and other violence should not be part of sports. (118)

vocational *adj.* pertaining to a job or career training. *Ex.* Those students are beginning vocational training in secretarial skills. (38)

warning *n.* caution. *Ex.* The police officer gave me a warning rather than an expensive speeding ticket. (162)

waste *n.* careless use. *Ex.* Buying that toy is a waste of money. (74)

weaken *v.* to cause someone to be not as strong as before. *Ex.* The illness weakened the elderly man. (56)

wealth *n.* a large amount of money. *Ex.* He inherited great wealth from his ancestors, who owned a huge estate. (36)

winner *n.* team or individual who is the best in competition. *Ex.* Who was the winner of the World Series this year? (109)

wish *v.* want; desire. *Ex.* I do not wish to go first in the competition. (84)

witch *n.* a woman who is believed to have special powers. *Ex.* There is a museum devoted to witches in Salem, Massachusetts. (140)

workload *n.* how much one is expected to do in one's job. *Ex.* You should speak with your boss if your workload is too demanding. (84)

workplace *n.* where people do their job. *Ex.* Is the atmosphere at your workplace casual or formal? (84)

worst *adj.* very bad *(superlative)*. *Ex.* I need to study hard for the exam because I do not want to get the worst grade in the class. (38)

wreak havoc *v.* cause great destruction. *Ex.* The storm wreaked havoc in the small town. (116)

zoom off *v.* to drive away quickly. *Ex.* After the holdup, the bank robbers zoomed off in their getaway car. (63)

Text Credits

"My Name" from *The House on Mango Street*. Copyright © 1984 by Sandra Cisneros. Published in the United States by Vintage Books, a division of Random House, Inc. New York, and distributed in Canada by Random House of Canada Limited, Toronto. Reprinted by permission of Susan Bergholz Literary Services, New York. Excerpt from *Iron & Silk* by Mark Salzman. Copyright © 1986 by Mark Salzman. Reprinted by permission of Random House, Inc. Excerpt reprinted by permission of the Putnam Publishing Group for *The Joy Luck Club* by Amy Tan. Copyright © 1989 by Amy Tan. Unpublished writing by Elsie Voltaire reprinted by permission of Elsie Voltaire. "The Game: A Life in Progress" (1991) by Jesse Lee Hardy reprinted by permission of Jesse Lee Hardy.

Photo Credits

Page x top: Lantos/The Picture Cube, center left: Thompson/The Picture Cube, center right: Siteman/The Picture Cube, bottom left: Eastcott/The Image Works, bottom right: Wood/The Picture Cube; p. 4, left: Wide World photos, right: Markel/Liaison International; p. 5: Rafael Millan; p. 10: Carroll/Stock Boston; p. 18, top: Dunn/The Picture Cube, bottom left: Craig/The Picture Cube, bottom right: Haspiel/Sigma; p. 32, top left: Maher/Stock Boston, top right: Nordell/The Picture Cube, center right: Snider The Image Works, bottom left: Velez The Image Works, bottom right: Ulrike Welsch; p. 34: Rowan/The Image Works; p. 37: Reuters/Bettmann; p. 42: Kirschenbaum/Stock Boston, p. 45: Rosenblum/The Picture Cube; p. 53: Menzel/Stock Boston; p. 55: Dorantes/Sygma; p. 66, top left: Collins/The Image Works, top right: Rios/Photo Researchers, center left: Kirschenbaum/Stock Boston, center right: Grey/Jeroboam, bottom: Ermahoff/The Image Works; p. 68: Fullman/The Picture Cube; p. 72: Frare/The Picture Cube; pgs. 80 and 83: Nogues/Sygma; p. 91: Nordell/The Picture Cube; p. 93: Newman, Photo Edit; p. 104, top: Austen/Stock Boston, center: Swyer/Stock Boston, center left: Lane/The Picture Cube, center right: Ulrike Welsch; p. 106: Lejeune/Stock Boston: p. 109: Bettmann; p. 117: Kullen/The Picture Cube; p. 118: Okoniewski/The Image Works; p. 123: *Lacrosse Playing Among the Sioux Indians,* 1851, oil on canvas, 28 1/4 x 40 3/4 in. (71.76 x 103.51 cm) in the Collection of the Corcoran Gallery of Art, Gift of William Wilson Corcoran; p. 126: Bettmann; p. 136, top: Ulrike Welsch, center: Fogle/The Picture Cube, bottom: Gatewood/Jeroboam; p. 138: illustration by Wanda Gag reprinted by permission of Coward-McCann from *Snow White and the Seven Dwarfs,* copyright 1938 by